SELL!

DALE CARNEGIE
& ASSOCIATES

SELL!

The Way Your Customers
Want to Buy

Published 2021 by Gildan Media LLC
aka G&D Media
www.GandDmedia.com

FIRST PAPERBACK EDITION 2021

Interior design by Meghan Day Healey of Story Horse, LLC

Library of Congress Cataloging-in-Publication Data is available upon request

ISBN: 978-1-7225-0536-3

10   9   8   7   6   5   4   3   2   1

*You can close more business in two months
by becoming interested in other people,
than you can in two years by trying
to get people interested in you.*
—DALE CARNEGIE

We would like to acknowledge the following contributors from Dale Carnegie & Associates who are quoted in this book.

- Joe Hart, *President and CEO*

- Dan Heffernan, *Chief Sales Officer*

- Noha El Daly, *Senior Director Sales and Global Master Trainer*

- David Wright, *Managing Partner, Austin and Houston, Texas*

- Jessie Wilson, *Senior Trainer and Consultant, Arkansas and Memphis, Tennessee*

- Dr. Greg Story, *Managing Partner, Tokyo, Japan*

- Matt Norman, *Managing Partner, Minnesota, Iowa, and Nebraska*

- Herb Escher, *Managing Partner, Rochester, New York*

- Rick Gallegos, *Managing Partner, Tampa, Florida*

- Jonathan Vehar, *Vice President, Product*

- Neville De Lucia, *Managing Partner, South Africa*

- John Rodgers, *Managing Partner, Pittsburgh and Cleveland*

- Pallavi Jha, *Managing Partner, India*

- Seth Mohorn, *Managing Partner, Arkansas and Memphis, Tennessee*

- Michael Crom, *Dale Carnegie & Associates Board of Directors*

- Terry Siebert, *Senior Partner, Madison, Wisconsin*

- Mark Marone, *Director Thought Leadership*

CONTENTS

PART ONE
Know Thyself

PART TWO

The Dale Carnegie Sales Process

PART THREE

Winning the Mental Game of Sales

PART FOUR

Bonus Material

FOREWORD

by Joe Hart

In 1995, I was a young attorney, and I had just taken my first Dale Carnegie course. I'd been interested in self-improvement ever since I read *How to Win Friends and Influence People*. My father had introduced me to Dale Carnegie and that book, but I really didn't know what to expect when I took the course. In the class, there was a woman who was so nervous that in the beginning she couldn't even stand up and say her name. By the end, she'd had a breakthrough and was much more confident.

The course changed my life too. Not just because I eventually became the CEO of Dale Carnegie Training, but it changed my life at the time. I saw myself differently afterward. I started my own business; I interacted with people differently. People were coming up to me and saying, "What happened to you, Joe? You're so much more confident!" I truly started living the Dale Carnegie principles.

Those are the very principles that are the foundation for *Sell!* They are learnable. I firmly believe that anyone can learn to sell. It's not some magical quality that you're either born with or not. Even if you have a natural talent for sales, having a process to use will make you much more effective, as you'll learn from some top salespeople in this book.

In an interview with *Japan Today** I said, "When I travel all over the world, people tell me about the impact Dale Carnegie has had on them, no matter what the language, culture, generation, ethnicity. It's pretty powerful. The core methodology—the way a Dale Carnegie course is taught—is the same. The way we certify our trainers and how our courses are delivered are the same. The thing that makes our training organization unique is that we do not import trainers. That means that our trainers inherently incorporate the local business context and practices. For example, in some cases, like in Japan, companies want to have Americanized training for their people because they do a lot of work outside Japan."

That is the essence of *Sell!* The book you hold in your hands will show you the same core principles that we teach around the world, the ones that have worked in our own organization and in thousands of others around the world. The beauty of the Dale Carnegie principles is that they are learnable, systematic, and customizable all at the same time. And they really help people to improve their lives. It's why I am so passionate about what we do.

---

* Chris Betros, "Dale Carnegie Training Stands the Test of Time," *Japan Times* website, Sept. 17, 2018: https://japantoday.com/category/features/executive-impact/Dale -Carnegie-Training-stands-the-test-of-time-new-technology.

DALE CARNEGIE: THE NEW GENERATION

(And Why You Should Read This Book!)

New York City, 1912

In the same year that the Titanic hit the iceberg, Dale Carnegie began teaching lessons in public speaking at the YMCA in New York City's Harlem district. He had persuaded the YMCA manager to allow him to instruct a class in return for 80 percent of the net proceeds.* Dale Carnegie had begun what would evolve into his classic human-relations course. The far-reaching success of his training ultimately led him to publish *How to Win Friends and Influence People* in 1936. Carnegie believed that if he could "help people realize their own unsuspected powers," he would not have lived in vain.

Clearly that was a long time ago. A lot in our world has changed. But there are just as many things that haven't

---

* "Dale Carnegie Discovered 'How to Win Friends and Influence People' in Harlem, 1911," *Harlem World* website, Nov. 26, 2017: https://www.harlemworldmagazine.com/dale-carnegie-discovered-win-friends-influence-people-harlem-1911.

changed. Dale Carnegie launched an entire personal-development industry and changed the way business books were written.

In fact, *How to Win Friends and Influence People* continues to be a best-seller, ranking as the eleventh best-selling book on Amazon of all time. Why is that? Why, in a world where there are 52 million books for sale on Amazon, does Dale Carnegie's classic stay fresh?

It's because some things never go out of fashion. Things like admitting when you're wrong, striving to make a good impression, and giving effective feedback are timeless ideas that need to be passed down from generation to generation. Human nature hasn't changed, nor have the principles for building trust, communicating effectively, and influencing and leading people. Carnegie's principles are timeless, and his formulas for leading an intentional, mindful, and successful life continue to be passed down from generation to generation.

Today Dale Carnegie's legacy is as strong as ever. With a roster of more than 8 million graduates, Dale Carnegie's 2000 professional trainers are passionately committed to unlocking the inherent potential of individuals, teams, and organizations in more than eighty-five countries and thirty languages.

New York City, late 2018
When I first started my career, I had always known I wanted to do something that was relationship-driven. I first started in an account-management and customer-success role at

the audio company Audible. I would work with customers after the contract was signed. I would make sure that they had everything they needed and that all problems were fixed or addressed. Eventually I was asked to take on more of a sales-hunting role in addition to the account management I was currently doing.

This was a bit scary for me for a few reasons. For one thing, public speaking absolutely terrified me. I would take those classes in college, get up in front of everyone, and completely freeze, and with sales there's a lot of addressing groups of people. It's giving your pitches and PowerPoint presentations and convincing potential clients about something they either need or want.

Second, I had always pictured salespeople as not being fully authentic or transparent. I didn't want to go into something where my quota, while important, meant putting customers second and pressuring them into buying something that wasn't right for them, knowing that eventually it would result in an angry customer—someone who would not stay around for the long run.

After a bit of thought, I decided to see what courses were out there to help me. I had heard of Dale Carnegie before, and after reading the reviews decided to find their sales course. I ended up choosing a three-day course in New York City, and decided this was the next step to figuring out if sales would be the right path for me.

As I was walking to class the first day, I remember being nervous. I thought I was going to be surrounded by salespeople who had been in the business for years. I didn't want to be the kid in class getting eye rolls because I was asking silly questions. I also had tons of questions running through my head: Is sales the direction my life is going to go in? Am I going to take this class and then reevaluate my entire career? Is Dale Carnegie going to turn me into a smooth-talking salesperson who can get anyone to buy anything at any cost?

After arriving in the classroom and talking with people, I had realized I had built up the people joining the class to be like the sharks from *Shark Tank*, but fortunately that wasn't the reality of the situation at all. I sat down with a group of great people; all of them were from different industries, with all types of sales experience.

Throughout the three days, my confidence in my sales skills boomed. I went from someone who thought I could never go into sales because it just wasn't me as a person to someone who was excited to go back to my company and take on this new challenge.

One of the points in Dale Carnegie's golden book to win people to your way of thinking is Principle 20: "Dramatize Your Ideas." This changed the way I sold. A few weeks after the class, I was working with a potential customer; after hearing all about their pain points, I knew my product was perfect for them. Through what I learned in my course, I was able to paint a picture for them of how my product would fix the pain points they had mentioned. Not only did this get them excited, but they increased the size of the deal, making them our largest client at the time.

I left Dale Carnegie not only knowing I wanted to go into sales but with a passion to take over the sales world. I went back to my company, ended up adding sales hunting to my résumé and within the first six months I was the top sales performer on the team and was promoted to sales manager.

Dale Carnegie helped me fine-tune my relationship skills, but also helped me put my passion for the products I sell into words in order to make others passionate as well. My Golden Book trophy has been on my desk since the day I won that challenge. It's a reminder to remember that I can be authentic and transparent while being a good salesperson, and for that I'll be eternally thankful.

—*Samantha Finan, sales professional, Audible*

Why Should You Read This Book?

You still might be asking, "Why do we need another book on sales? There are already hundreds out there on the market. What is new under the sun?"

First, you can grow your earning power by learning ideas and methods that are the original, the G.O.A.T. (greatest of all time). Everything else on the market came after Dale Carnegie, and much of it is derived from his work. Carnegie training programs have been offered and have evolved over 100 years. Today they are delivered in thirty-five languages and eighty-five countries around the world.

Are there graphics and models and useful forms? Yes.

But this book has something you won't find in any other book: real stories from our top sales professionals and our highest-rated professional sales trainers, who don't get to train unless they've been in the trenches.

Think we're exaggerating? No matter where you sign up for a Dale Carnegie training program—Algeria, England, Trinidad and Tobago, France, Cyprus, Japan, Romania, Germany, Mauritius, Brazil, Tunisia, pretty much anywhere you go on earth, from the tiniest countries to the biggest—Dale Carnegie sales professionals and trainers are there. Dale Carnegie trainers work with thousands of companies in every imaginable industry. Chances are, you've bought something from a salesperson using our method, and didn't even realize it.

What does this mean for you? It means that we know—and you'll learn in this book—why having coffee in a sales meeting in Qatar has nothing to do with coffee. You'll discover what it means when a prospect says yes in Japan. (Hint: It doesn't mean you've made the sale.)

Second, you'll learn exactly what your customers and prospects are saying they want from you as a sales professional—and it's not what some current books or provocative sales gurus claim. That's because our new research challenges some of the ideas and sales approaches popularized in recent years, which diminish the importance of relationships, trust, and personal effectiveness.

Third, you can become a top performer by learning how sales follow a predictable pattern that you can harness to sell more. Buyers in all industries have changed their habits by researching information that is now readily and quickly accessible—shifting more power to them to make the right decisions. They are better informed and more confident before you're even engaged. The Carnegie sales model will teach you the skills you need at each buying stage to earn the trust, confidence, and respect of your buyers.

Finally, you'll learn principles that will help you not only in sales but in your personal and professional life, regardless of where you are in your lifelong learning journey. Dale Carnegie's principles are listed at the beginning and referenced throughout the book. Examples include principle 17: "Try honestly to see things from the other person's point of view" and principle 8: "Talk in terms of the other person's interest." They will make you stop, think, assess yourself, and do things differently so that you can achieve both your sales and personal goals.

After all, that's why you bought this book, right?

FIVE THINGS THIS BOOK WILL HELP YOU ACHIEVE

(That Aren't About Sales)

1. Increase your influence.
2. Become a better storyteller.
3. Increase your confidence.
4. Handle complaints, criticism, and negative feedback with ease.
5. Build stronger relationships.

DALE CARNEGIE'S THIRTY PRINCIPLES

Build Trust in Your Relationships

1. Don't criticize, condemn, or complain.
2. Give honest and sincere appreciation.
3. Arouse in the other person an eager need or want.
4. Become genuinely interested in other people.
5. Smile.
6. Remember that a person's name is to that person the sweetest and most important sound in any language.
7. Be a good listener. Encourage others to talk about themselves.
8. Talk in terms of the other person's interests.
9. Make the other person feel important—and do it sincerely.

Influence Others: Win People to Your Way of Thinking

10. The only way to get the best of an argument is to avoid it.
11. Show respect for other person's opinions. Never say, "You're wrong."

12. If you are wrong, admit it quickly and emphatically.
13. Begin in a friendly way.
14. Get the other person saying "Yes, yes" immediately.
15. Let the other person do a great deal of the talking.
16. Let the other person feel that the idea is his or hers.
17. Try honestly to see things from the other person's point of view.
18. Be sympathetic to the other person's ideas and desires.
19. Appeal to the other, nobler motives.
20. Dramatize your ideas.
21. Throw down a challenge.

Be a Leader

22. Begin with praise and honest appreciation.
23. Call attention to people's mistakes indirectly.
24. Talk about your own mistakes before criticizing the other person.
25. Ask questions instead of giving direct orders.
26. Let the other person save face.
27. Praise the slightest improvement, and praise every improvement. Be "hearty in your approbation and lavish in your praise."
28. Give the other person a fine reputation to live up to.
29. Use encouragement. Make the fault seem easy to correct.
30. Make the other person happy about doing the thing you suggest.

HOW TO GET THE MOST OUT OF THIS BOOK

Just as Dale Carnegie wrote a chapter on how to get the most out of *How to Win Friends and Influence People*, we've found it's useful as readers to have some tips on how to get the most out of this book. Why? Because reading something isn't enough to change our performance.

So here are our tips:

1. Change your performance with our proven three-step process as you read the book. We call it the *performance change pathway.*™

   • **Assess yourself.** No one changes unless they really want to change. Your pathway to top performance starts with the simple realization that unless you're emotionally ready to change, you probably won't. You bought this book, so you have a desire to get better. Now as you read this book, you'll be provided with opportunities to assess your attitudes and skills. If you're ready, you'll be honest with yourself. Top salespeople usually begin on their path to the top when they realize it takes adopting a mind-set of "why not me?" coupled with a desire to constantly improve and honestly assess themselves. Why *not* you?

- **Experience learning.** Taking a Dale Carnegie training program is intense and effective, and millions of graduates call their programs a life-changing learning experience. But reading this book can change your life too, as long as you try out what we recommend. So practice what you're learning here and then try it in the real world. Ask a trusted mentor or your boss for feedback as you try out new skills, or team up with peers to learn together. To experience learning, you need that honest social experience.

- **Sustain your learning.** It's easy to forget what you learn and fall back into old patterns. Schedule time for yourself right now, on your calendar, every day or two to practice new skills and approaches recommended in this book. Ask your immediate manager for input. Tell her or him your goals and dreams, and ask for help. You'll be surprised at how people around you will support you when you become vulnerable and work constantly to improve.

2. Read the last page of each chapter first. It's the overview of key concepts. This doesn't mean that if you already

think you know what's in the chapter, you can skip it. Each chapter is filled with stories and tips you'll find useful even if you understand the basic ideas. But by starting with a summary before beginning, you will be sustaining your learning as you read the chapter for the first time—killing two birds with one stone!

3. Then go back and read the chapter. If you're using a Kindle or other e-reader, feel free to liberally use its highlighter feature and bookmarks. Even if you never go back and look at the things again, highlighting and bookmarking tells your brain, "This is important. Remember this." If you've got a paper book, mark away to your heart's content. This is YOUR book. Write notes, fold pages, make smiley faces and emojis on the thing. Don't think of it as some precious manual that's to be preserved. Think of it as a workbook.

4. Stop at the end of each chapter and ask yourself if it's better to reread the chapter or move on to the next one. Sometimes the instant repetition of reading it again plants the information deeper into your brain.

5. Tell other people about what you read. Describing the ideas to someone else is a great way to solidify what you're learning.

6. When you're done with the book, read it again. You can just look at your bookmarked and highlighted passages, or you can read the whole thing from cover

to cover again—whatever's your style. But just as you probably watched those episodes of *The Office* over and over again, reading this book numerous times will allow you to relate to the material differently each time.

7. Finally, relate the content to your life. As you read the stories, ask yourself, "What would I have done in that situation? Has something like that ever happened to me?" Learn from your mistakes, applaud your successes, and focus on constantly improving yourself.

8. Post your greatest takeaways from each chapter with the hashtag #DaleCarnegieTraining using Facebook, Twitter, Instagram, or LinkedIn. By "teaching" others, you'll retain the skills faster!

As Dale Carnegie said, "Knowledge isn't power until it's applied."

Part One

Know Thyself

1. WHAT ARE YOU SELLING?

Mike Peters was dejected by the time he got back to his car. *What am I doing wrong?* he wondered. He'd thought he'd done all the right things to make the sale. It's not as if he was new at the sales game. He'd been doing it for twenty years. But more and more often lately, Mike had been going back to his car at the end of the sales call with the "We'll think about it and get back to you" refrain that he knew to be the kiss of death to closing the sale.

Starting the car, he mentally went over the meeting. He'd built rapport by talking about the things he'd seen in the prospect's office and on his LinkedIn profile. He'd asked questions to reveal the prospect's goals and challenges and asked more questions to guide him to feeling the need to make a change. He'd presented his product as the solution to the prospect's problem, overcome objections, explained the features of the product, and tied them to each of the prospect's pain points. Then, when he felt the time was right, he'd asked for the sale. That was the way he'd been taught, and it was the way he'd made sales consistently throughout his modestly successful career.

Getting on the highway back to the office, Mike already knew how it was going to play out. He'd follow up with the prospect, thanking him for his time and offering to answer any questions. But by the time he'd gotten to the car, he knew that the sale was lost. The guy was probably on the Internet right now, looking for a cheaper, faster solution than the one Mike had offered.

Shaking his head in frustration, Mike said aloud, to no one in the car, "I hope you're happy, random Amazon seller. I did all the hard work for you, and you're the one who will get the sale."

Now you're probably reading this and going over in your mind what you might have done differently. You might be thinking, "I'd have sent the follow-up while I was still in the car." Or "He must have rushed the process. It's about developing a relationship."

You might be right. In fact, you *are* right. But that's not why Mike lost the sale. Mike lost the sale because he forgot what he was truly selling. What are *you* really selling?

Is it a product or service?

Is it a solution to your customer's problems? Is it a relationship?

We believe the answer is no. You may end up selling those things. But the underlying thing that you are selling—the thing that can differentiate you from every other salesperson on the planet—is *trust*.

"Oh, yeah. I've heard this before. Trust sells. I get that."
Let's dig deeper, though. What does it mean to say you
trust someone? And what are you trusting them to do?
Think about it in your own personal life. Who are the people you trust? You most likely have a high level of trust in
your intimate relationships, with your mate, your children,
and your family. But what does it really mean when you
say, "I trust you"? Trust means that you believe that the
other person is going to tell you the truth, even if it doesn't
benefit them. It means that you can count on them to do
what they say they are going to do, when they are going
to do it, and in the manner they said they would. Ask the
long-standing top salesperson in your organization, and
they will tell you they pass up on customers who don't truly
need what they're selling. Their reputation is more important than a quick sale that creates problems for a customer.

What Exactly Is Trust?

At Dale Carnegie Training, we asked customers around
the world how they would describe trust in their salesperson, and their responses overwhelmingly validate what
we've said above. The top two answers to our open-ended
question, "How would you define trust?" centered on two
themes: "I can believe them; they are honest, credible and
knowledgeable" (50 percent) and "They are looking out for
my best interest and providing value" (25 percent).

Customers gave salespeople clear-cut advice in this
latest research. When asked about the important behaviors that drive trust, more than 85 percent of customers in

the study said that among a salesperson's most important behaviors for building trust are:

1. "Providing honest and complete information."
2. "Doing what's right for me rather than trying to make the sale."
3. "Keeping their promises."

As one survey respondent put it, trust in a salesperson "means I can count on them to give me straightforward answers, even if they may lose the sale because of it."

Mayer et al.* defined *trust* as "the willingness of a party to be vulnerable to the actions of another party based on the expectation that the other will perform a particular action important to the trustor, irrespective of the ability to monitor or control that other party."

This is just a formal way of saying what we said in the beginning. Customers want to know that they can trust you to be honest about what you can (and cannot) do, then to actually *do it,* in the way you said you would, and to have their best interest at heart when you do it.

So what are you selling when you get a prospect to trust you? You're selling *yourself.* You're conveying authenticity and transparency. You are a person whose job it is to solve problems, and what makes you unique are the solutions you come up with.

---

* Roger C. Mayer, James H. Davis, and F. David Schoorman, "An Integrative Model of Organizational Trust," *The Academy of Management Review* 20, no. 3 (July 1995): 709–34.

The Know Thyself Self-Appraisal

Try this exercise. Get out a piece of paper, or open a new document on your computer, and set a timer for five minutes. In five minutes, write down every answer you can think of to the question, "Why should anyone trust me?" Don't just skip over this exercise to get to what everyone else said. Really do it. OK—go.

Need some help? We'll give you some prompts. Here is "The Know Thyself Self-Appraisal." These questions can help you write your answers.

Interaction with Others
- Are you a naturally reserved person, who prefers to let others take the conversational lead?
- Are you more outgoing and accessible?
- Are you an analytic, logical thinker?
- Do you like to tell stories and anecdotes to get your ideas across?

Physical Appearance
- Are you a large, gregarious person in body and in voice?
- Are you someone who doesn't immediately attract a lot of notice?

Since this is a chapter on trust, we are obviously trusting that you did the exercise. Five minutes was a long time, wasn't it?

What did you discover? If you're like most people, the exercise started out with the kinds of answers that come easily. "People should trust me because I am honest. I believe in my product and that it's the best one on the market." (More later on what to do if you don't really believe in what you're selling.)

But after a couple of minutes, you probably ran out of ideas. That's when the real answers start to come out. "People should trust me because I have always been a trustworthy person. Even as a child, I was the one my parents could count on to take care of my little brother. Taking care of other people is important to me. When someone trusts you to do something, that's the most important thing they can give you."

This exercise can really help you uncover your core values as they relate to trust. Maybe you were let down by someone else, and so you don't believe that trust is ever really possible. Or maybe it made you more determined to be trustworthy. Or did you learn to trust again?

Maybe you realized you haven't always been the most trustworthy person. "Honestly? People shouldn't trust me. I've been known to lie at times to get what I want." It's OK if you wrote stuff like that, because it means you're getting real. It means you're being honest with yourself about where you can improve, and that's a good thing. This is the no-judgment zone here.

Whatever you wrote and discovered about yourself as a trustworthy person, that's your foundation. That is the groundwork for everything you do in sales and in life. You have to trust yourself before anyone else will trust you.

The Way You Do One Thing
Is the Way You Do Everything

We all benefit by asking ourselves this question: Do we value being a person who is worthy of other people's trust? We might think, "Of course!" But do we act like it? There's an old saying: "The way you do one thing is the way you do everything." So ask yourself: Do you behave in a trustworthy manner all day, or only when you're trying to make a sale? If you see $20 lying on the ground, do you pocket it or do you try and find its owner? If you say, "I'll call you tomorrow," do you? Or do you make excuses for why you didn't call?

Trust is, at its core, a matter of integrity. Sales is often perceived as a sleazy business because salespeople are at times perceived as having a lack of integrity. "She'll promise anything to make the sale." "When I walk onto a car lot, the salesperson isn't trying to sell me the car that's best for me; he's trying to sell the car that most needs to be sold." That's the perception that we at Dale Carnegie Training have been working to overcome for more than 100 years.

Let's look at two scenarios, one where trust is at the foundation of the sale and one where it isn't.

Karen lost her husband of twenty years to cancer two years ago. She and her kids moved from the family home to a beautiful condo by the beach. It was soothing to her soul to see the ocean waves lapping ashore as she sat on her deck every morning. The family dog, Salty, would lie at her feet as she watched the cruise ships go by. One thing she had talked about with her husband was taking a cruise among the Hawaiian Islands. Karen obviously couldn't take the trip with her husband, but she could still make incredible memories with her kids. So she booked a twenty-one-day cruise. Her kids were so excited! "But who is going to watch Salty and my fish?" her daughter asked. "Are you really going to trust a stranger to come into our home?" her son questioned. Salty was thirteen years old and needed her kidney medicine twice a day. She had to be fed a special diet and to be let outside on a specific schedule. Karen clearly needed to find someone she could trust to care for her animals and her home.

The first person she interviewed was Casey. She was a twenty-one-year-old college student whom Karen had found on a pet-sitting site. Walking in and seeing the 180-degree ocean view, Casey said, "Wow, this is quite a view. You must have some killer parties here." When Salty came up and licked her, she bent down and pet her, but her eyes kept looking around at the condo. The whole time Casey was there, she kept thinking about how great it would be to stay there: *I can have coffee on the deck every morning. Maybe do some yoga.* "You are really lucky to live here," she said. As Karen was explaining the tasks involved, she wondered if Casey was even listening. She just kept walking from room to room, looking at the view. As the interview ended, Karen told Casey she was interviewing several others and would get back to her. The fact was, while Casey looked fine on paper, there was something missing.

The second person Karen interviewed was Olivia. She was a fifty-year-old woman whose own kids had gone to visit their father over spring break, and she'd wanted to get out of her own home to distract herself. As she walked in, the first thing she did was bend down and talk to Salty. "Hi, girl. How are you?" Olivia wisely recognized that Karen's first concern was going to be how well she bonded with Salty. She made a conscious decision *not* to comment on the view or the condo. She wasn't there to admire the view or the home. She was there to solve a problem, and the problem was "What do I do about caring for my animals when I'm gone?" In order to make this sale, Olivia knew that she needed to demonstrate that she was worthy of Karen's trust. Olivia put herself in Karen's shoes. *What would I be feeling if I had just lost my husband and I were going away from home with my kids for three weeks? What would matter to me?* Karen and Olivia sat down on the couch and talked. Olivia asked questions about the trip, about how to care for Salty, and about the fish. Her whole focus was on helping Karen to see that she could trust her. Whether or not she could have coffee or do yoga on the deck was secondary.

It's pretty clear from these scenarios which woman got the job. Was it because Olivia was more qualified? No: Casey had come highly recommended on the pet-sitting site. She was a college student, had shown up to the interview on time, and had done all the right things. Except one. She hadn't realized that what she was really selling was trust.

Risky Business

Whenever someone trusts someone else, there is risk involved. The person doing the trusting is, at some level, vulnerable to the person being trusted. It can be small, like trusting that the charger you buy is going to work for more than a week before breaking. Or it can be large, like trusting someone to care for your elderly father or grandfather in his nursing home.

Risking being vulnerable is what makes trust different than some other forms of human interaction, such as confidence or cooperation. You can have confidence in someone or cooperate with them without being vulnerable to their actions.

In the sales relationship, the buyer is taking a risk to believe you. He or she is trusting that the solution to the problem will be as you promised. You could, if you were a less trustworthy person, take advantage of the buyer. The only thing you have to lose is the sale. If you violate their trust, the buyer loses much more. They lose the solution to their problem, yes. But they also lose respect: respect for you, respect for your brand, and even respect for themselves as a person who can tell whether or not a person is trustworthy.

Karen, in our scenario, is taking a risk. She is vulnerable to the person she chooses to take care of her animals. She must trust that they will be kept healthy and that the person who watches them is being honest about their skill level and will do what they say they will do, when they say they'll do it, and how it is supposed to be done.

So what determines whether a customer will be able to trust a salesperson? There are three dimensions of trust. They are *integrity*, *ability*, and *benevolence*.

Integrity is being honest.
- What will motivate or guide your performance?
- Are you able to express your performance principles?
- Can you state what you *wouldn't* do because you find it wrong on principle?
- Is this set of principles one that others would agree with?

Ability is doing what you say you will do in the way you say it will be done.
- Can you do what you say you will do?
- Do you have a track record of performance in the area required?
- What evidence supports your claim to competency and ability in the domain of concern?

Benevolence is the ability to help someone for reasons other than profit.
- Do you understand the other's situation?
- Do you hold the other's interests as dear as your own?
- Are you seeking to make the other person's life better?
- Are the actions you will take in the best interest of the other?

A trust-based relationship is the foundation to sales. It is both an outcome and a driver of trust. In other words, when you have a trusting relationship, it builds more trust. Your customers aren't just customers. They are people.

People with their own dreams and aspirations and, yes, problems. When you make a sale, you are making a difference in the life of a person.

Noha El Daly, senior director of sales and global master trainer for Dale Carnegie & Associates, talks about the time it can take to build trust. The global head of sales for another organization "was discussing his global strategy change and asking for input," says El Daly, "and we spent the majority of the meeting discussing his plans before starting to discuss the learning journey. He mentioned on several occasions that we would not need this in the training room but that he needed my perspective to finalize the strategy prior to the training. This level of being a trusted advisor was ignited from a meeting where we used principle 4: 'Become genuinely interested in other people,' and its power was felt. The client felt then that we are true partners and not just a training provider. It took long hours of discussing the business—long hours of unbilled work. But this is the investment that we make in our business. Consultative selling is not just a process; it is a state of mind."

At Dale Carnegie, we believe that effective selling requires productive relationships built on reciprocal trust between the buyer and seller that comes from established credibility and a mutual understanding of value. As effective salespeople, we need to move from being product pushers (someone who is focused on his or her own desire to sell products) to being a trusted advisor (someone who can be trusted to advise the customer in a way that is best for the customer).

Product Pusher ⟶ **Trusted Advisor**

Building Trust with the Dale Carnegie Principles

Here are some of Dale Carnegie's principles about building trusting relationships. Here's the secret—it's not about you! That's right, it's about the people around you. Read each one of these principles. Practice just one for an entire day in each interaction. On the next day, practice a different principle. Prepare to be astonished as people gravitate to you!

1. Don't criticize, condemn, or complain.
2. Give honest and sincere appreciation.
3. Arouse in the other person an eager need or want.
4. Become genuinely interested in other people.
5. Smile.
6. Remember that a person's name is to that person the sweetest and most important sound in any language.
7. Be a good listener. Encourage others to talk about themselves.
8. Talk in terms of the other person's interests.
9. Make the other person feel important—and do it sincerely.

In this chapter we've talked about the first of the three elements of successful selling—trust. In the next chapter, we'll look at the second element of effective selling—credibility.

The Bottom Line for Chapter 1

- The best sales process in the world will not work unless it is based on a foundation of reciprocal trust-based relationships between the seller and the buyer.
- Our latest research shows customers want three things from you:
  1. To provide honest and complete information.
  2. To do what's right for them rather than trying to make the sale.
  3. To keep your promises.

Did you assess yourself? In order for you to garner someone else's trust, you have to know why you are trustworthy.
- Trust involves risk and vulnerability.
- The way you do one thing is the way you do everything.
- The three dimensions of trust are *integrity*, *ability*, and *benevolence*.
- Practice the first set of Dale Carnegie principles.

Seventy-one percent of buyers say they would rather have a salesperson they "completely trusted" than one that gave them the "best price."

2. PERSONAL CREDIBILITY

"I have eight weeks of money left before I go bankrupt, and you're telling me I need to give you two weeks of that?" This is what Bill—a gentleman who had recently launched his own environmental-consulting firm, had told Dale Carnegie managing partner Dave Wright after asking him to meet for coffee at Starbucks. Bill had described his need to attend sales training, and Dave had simply described the eight weekly three-hour sessions and the related investment.

Years later, Dave says, "I felt deep empathy—I could tell he was in pain. So for me this was a major gut check in my life. How much do I believe in this—how deeply? This guy will go bankrupt faster if it doesn't work. Having already built trust with him, I said 'Bill, if it's six weeks or eight weeks, what's the difference? You'll fail unless you do something to change it.' I had faith in our program and our principles. By the fourth week of the program, Bill learned to use credibility statements to get appointments and to ask more effective questions. He obtained two very high-level meetings and closed a deal that covered his revenue goal for a year. Bill reached out to me recently from his San Francisco office, one of two locations of his now thriving firm."

Relationship selling. That's the key. How many times have you heard that? We've heard it so many times from so many different places that it's become one of those buzzwords like "paradigm" and "game changer" and "best practices" that no one even listens to anymore: "This paradigm shift is a real game changer. We need to incorporate relationship selling into our best practices."

But what does that actually mean? We have an entire sales course on the topic of relationship selling, so obviously we believe in the concept. But we look at it a little differently than you might think.

Buyers these days are savvy, and risk-averse. When someone unfamiliar comes to our door, when they call us on the phone or send an email, our first reaction is "What do you want?" We may say it nicely, "How can I help you?" But really we're thinking, "Why are you here and what do you want?"

If someone comes in and starts "relationship selling" to you, you're going to know it and the walls are going to go up. You're not going to risk trusting someone you suspect is only in the relationship so that they can sell you something. Are we saying that relationships aren't the vehicle for sales? Not at all. It's the name of our sales course for a reason. What we are saying is that in order to do relationship selling, you have to be in a relationship *first*. They have to trust you *first*, and then you can explore a sale.

This is where credibility comes in. Like trust, credibility must be earned over time. If your business is transactional in nature (such as retail or the restaurant industry), then your credibility comes from the business brand. People go to McDonald's because the company has demonstrated credibility over the years, and customers can trust that they are going to get what they expect when they eat there. Consistency is a key element of credibility.

If your business is *not* transactional, then the credibility becomes personal. It becomes about who you are as a person. Your traits, your attitudes, your personality all become part of your personal brand. Just as a company promotes a brand, you do too.

Selling Is a Form of Leadership

It might surprise you to think that selling is a form of leadership, but it is. Think about what a leader does. Leaders see a destination and then develop a strategy to get there. They then influence others to take the actions necessary to get to the destination. The followers *trust* the leader to get them there.

Now think about what salespeople do. They see a solution to a buyer's problem and develop a strategy to get there. Then they influence the buyer to take the actions necessary to get to the destination of not having the problem anymore. Your buyer has to trust you to help them solve their problem.

Credibility is a cornerstone of leadership. If people don't believe in you, they aren't going to follow you anywhere.

Ask the Right Kinds of Questions

So how can we begin to develop credibility? In addition to personal characteristics like being respectful and having demonstrable professional competence, it comes from asking the right questions. Notice we're saying the *right* questions. Asking the wrong questions is often worse than not asking questions at all. It can kill our credibility before your mouth is even shut.

For example, Stacy Watson was car shopping, and like many people, she hated the entire process. She'd done a lot of research online and had talked to friends and family. She had it narrowed down to three cars and walked into a dealership that carried one of them so that she could test-drive it. She was interested in horsepower and engine size and wanted to see for herself how quickly she could accelerate and stop.

Lee, a salesperson in the dealership that day, saw Stacy looking at one of the cars. "That's a pretty one, isn't it? It's one of our more popular models." When she didn't answer, he probed further. "What color are you interested in? This particular one comes in five different color combinations, and you can choose between leather or fabric."

In Stacy's mind, Lee instantly lost all credibility. Why? Because it appeared to her that he was giving her the features like color and fabric choice because she was a woman. *If I were a man,* she thought, *he'd probably be telling me about torque and suspension.*

In Lee's mind, he was demonstrating product knowledge and thought he was building credibility by talking about the things he thought she would be interested in.

Clearly asking some questions rather than prejudging buyers leads to more trust.

On the other hand, you can build credibility quickly by applying principle 4: "Become genuinely interested in other people," and principle 8: "Talk in terms of the other person's interest."

Jessie Wilson, a senior trainer and consultant for Dale Carnegie in Arkansas, was in her first year with Carnegie when she discovered a company whose published corporate values matched her own and those of her local office. Intrigued, she made a cold call looking for a decision maker. With her first contact, Jessie spoke in terms of the company's interest and was genuinely impressed by the fact that he listened intently and asked questions rather than brushing her off. He was not a decision maker, but Jessie followed up with a heartfelt, handwritten thank-you note saying that even if they didn't work together, she was leaving the interaction with a clear impression that he was living and following their corporate values. He responded via email and said he was blown away by her thank you note and included the contact information for the decision maker, Steve. Furthermore, he had already reached out to Steve telling him to expect Jessie's call.

Jessie called Steve a week later and after a brief fifteen-minute phone call, they sketched out the beginning of a long-term contract. In essence, Jessie skipped through most phases of the selling process purely because of her credibility and ability to establish trusting relationships!

Knowing the right questions to ask, and how to ask them, is highly dependent on the person being asked. Different demographics, different personality types, and even different cultures all have different norms for question asking. Do it the wrong way and we risk credibility instantly.

Millennials and young people increasingly want their questions answered online rather than in person (and by *in person* we mean live—either on the phone or face-to-face). If you're one of them and you're reading this, you know what we mean. Who answers the phone anymore unless they know who's calling?

Introverts and people with social anxiety are going to be less receptive than others to questions they may find intrusive. People with a direct communication style aren't going to want the pleasantries that sometimes precede conversation. "Get to the point" is the mantra of this style. But indirect communicators will be put off and even offended if you get right to the point.

Cultural differences influence the way we ask questions as well. Greg Story, president of Dale Carnegie in Tokyo, Japan, says:*

> In Japan, a lot of buyers expect to control proceedings, such that the seller turns up, gives their pitch, and then the buyer happily shoots it full of holes. What Japanese buyers are doing is trying to ascertain the risk factor of what you are proposing by disparaging everything you have just said. They now want you to provide answers that eliminate their fears. You

---

* Dr. Greg Story, "The Sales Japan Series," Apple podcasts website, accessed April 28, 2019: https://itunes.apple.com/us/podcast/the-sales-japan-series-by-dale-carnegie-training-japan/id1172353048?mt=2.

are immediately on the back foot. The client, not you, is controlling the sales process.

To break this pattern (which has a very low success rate), we need to ask pertinent questions and find out what they really need. In order to do that, we need to get their permission to ask questions. This transition into the questioning part of the sales process is absolutely critical. Don't miss this: in Japan the buyer is of supreme importance. Hence buyers here may feel our questions are impertinent, intrusive and unnecessary, so we must gain their permission to proceed. Every single time I have been forced to just give my pitch—because the buyer has denied me the opportunity to ask questions—there has been no sale achieved. We need to be better skilled, to get them to allow us to fully understand how we can best serve them. That is why we need to be asking questions and listening carefully to their answers. So that we can make that transition, after saying "Maybe we could do the same for you?" we softly mention, "In order to help me understand if we can do that or not, would you mind if I asked a few questions?" We say this almost as a throwaway line; no big deal, nothing to see here. When they agree, we are now free to explore in detail their current situation, what they aspire to, what is holding them back and what would success mean to them personally. If you don't ask these questions, you have little chance of convincing the client you can help them solve their problems.

Noha El Daly, senior director of sales and global master trainer for Dale Carnegie & Associates says:

> Establishing rapport is key to relationship selling, yet it means different things to different people. If you go to Northern Europe, we start the meeting with short pleasantries, yet going straight to the agenda items is considered a sign of respect that should be taken into consideration. On the other hand, in Northern Africa, one can spend a good part of the meeting asking about the family, the person's health, specifically about their children, if we know that they have a family, their work. And it would be an endless list of "*ça va*?"—*ça va*? meaning "OK?"—and prior to that, you would fill in the blanks regarding who or what you are asking about. The first time you attend a meeting like this, you wonder if the other person is completely insane. I remember many years ago when I was in Morocco, I went to a client along with a local salesperson and we spent at least seven minutes asking the question over and over again to ensure that everybody in the client's family was OK! But if you don't spend enough time with the personal questions, it means you're not interested.
>
> In other markets, like the Arabian Gulf countries, they are more private, and therefore inquiring so much about one's family when one does not know the person well would be considered inappropriate, especially if there people in the room that the client meets for the first time.

I was once in a meeting in Qatar, and the minute I went in the office, I was offered a cup of local coffee, which is very heavy on spices. Whether one is a coffee drinker or not, this does not matter to the hosts, who expect that the guests appreciate the gesture and drink their coffee. The coffee is a special blend with cardamom, and it is the pride of the host to flaunt how special the coffee is. I am not a coffee drinker, and the Arabian coffee is too strong for my taste buds, but this is a moment when I had to convince my taste buds that it was not time to be fussy. I drank the coffee, and it was only then that the host started discussing business.

It is important to note that it is a cultural norm to open any business subject only once the guest has savored their coffee. Understanding and accepting the local culture is key for relationship selling. Relationship here is the one of trust that one establishes from the very beginning to demonstrate that we come not to impose our ways but to accept the client's way of doing things.

What does this mean for us as salespeople? It means that to be credible as a salesperson, we need to be aware of the social norms around asking questions in the culture we're operating, the personality and communication style of the person we're talking to, and the medium in which they prefer to talk. We'll have tips and suggestions on how to do that in the application sections of this book.

Just as we've said that for a person to trust us, we have to trust ourselves, the same thing is true with credibility. We have to own it before we can sell it!

To generate interest from your buyer and quickly establish credibility in a sales meeting, develop a *credibility statement.* This is a brief passage that helps you clarify what it is you do and how it helps your customers. You'll notice that this is designed to be shared with the client or prospect. Please note, we aren't recommending you whip out your credibility statement and read it. It's simply a framework for verbally establishing credibility in the sales environment.

In other words, your credibility statement is what demonstrates your leadership in getting customers from point A to point B. It's what you say before you ask them if it's OK to ask questions. Otherwise you risk coming off like that guy on Facebook who asks overly personal questions when you don't even know him in real life.

Elements of a Credibility Statement*

You can immediately see a change in your results by using this simple approach:

1. Cite general benefits your solution provides that relate to the customer's needs, wants, and issues.
2. Give results of how specific clients have benefited.
3. Suggest that similar benefits are possible.
4. Transition to the next step.

---

* "Credibility Statement: How to Build Credibility?" Dale Carnegie Lessons website, accessed April 28, 2019: http://dalecarnegielesson.blogspot.com/2011/06/credibility-statement.html.

To draft your own credibility statement, begin by stating in general what value you bring to customers. You can use your mission statement to figure this out. State your company's mission as briefly as possible—less than ten words is ideal. If your company does not have one, create your own. Some tips for good mission statements might be:

• Be brief and memorable.
• Use creative language.
• Affirm what you do for your clients.
• Capture imagination.

Examples: "We preserve memories" (photo processing). "We create wealth" (financial planning). "We build and retain business relationships" (training).

1. **Results**. This is the heart of the credibility statement. Cite specific results you have helped your clients achieve. The more specific you are, the more convincing you will be. To do this, you have to know your customers well and how they are benefiting from doing business with you. Some guidelines for citing results:

• Be accurate. This is not the time to overstate capabilities.
• Be specific. Use dollars, percentages, cost savings, time saved.
• Be precise. 23.2 percent is more credible than 25 percent.
• Use your client's name if you have permission and they are respected.

Examples: "We've helped a company in your industry increase revenue per rep by 20 percent." We helped a similar company cut costs by over $1 million using our software to replace manual process."

2. **State That Similar Results are Possible**, but use understatement. Don't promise miraculous results. The buyer may be thinking that their company is different, that their situation is unique, or that you are exaggerating. The best way to overcome their initial doubt is to understate.

Examples: "I can't promise you these results until I know more about your needs." Or "You may find your results would be higher, lower." Or "You may be able to see a similar return on your investment."

3. **Advance**. By now you should have earned the attention of the buyer. Buyers rarely hear salespeople say that we can't promise them the world. The last step is to advance to the next level of the sale. We need to ask questions to see if we have a solution for them. This is a good time to start moving the buyer to yes. Ask permission to advance the sale.

Examples: "To see whether we might have a solution for you, may I ask a few questions?" "Can I get some details from you to see if we have a fit?" "Would you tell me some of your needs that I have not seen from your website?"

Why Does This Work?

Credibility statements work because of Dale Carnegie principle 8—you're talking in terms of the buyer's interest. Nobody cares about your products or services. They only care about what they can do for them. So one of the best ways to establish credibility is by talking about issues relevant to the customer. These issues should reflect what similar customers have enjoyed by using your solution.

Here again are the steps and some examples:
1. Cite general benefits your solution provides that relate to the customer's needs, wants, and issues.
2. Give results of how specific clients have benefited.
3. Suggest that similar benefits are possible.
4. Transition to the next step.

Example:

Step 1. Other companies in your industry have been able to increase their company's revenues and reduce operating expenses by web-enabling some of their general business practices.

Step 2. ABC Online has told us they have strengthened their web presence and have sold more to existing accounts by 27 percent.

Step 3. Perhaps your company could realize the same benefits. Let's find twenty minutes to sit down together and find out.

Step 4. I'll call your office at 9:00 Tuesday to schedule a time for us to talk.

Again, credibility statements work because they are brief and get you talking in terms of the other person's interests. The biggest mistake we see here is salespeople doing the opposite and launching into too much information about themselves—*their* company, *their* products. Remember, it's not about you, it's about them!

In the first chapter, we said that effective selling requires productive relationships built on reciprocal trust between the buyer and seller that comes from established credibility and a mutual understanding of value. In this chapter, we've talked about the second of those elements, which is credibility. Next, we'll get into the third element, which is the mutual understanding of value.

The Bottom Line for Chapter 2

- Sales is a form of leadership and uses many of the same skills.
- Asking the wrong questions is worse than asking no questions at all, because it can destroy your credibility instantly.
- To ask the right questions, you need to factor in things like communication style, personality, and cultural norms.
- Use a credibility statement to spark interest and quickly gain initial credibility, then ask permission to ask questions.
- Use one of the Dale Carnegie principles each day. Write down in a journal or Evernote or your iPhone memo what you learned each day. Go back each week and reflect on your learnings.
- What is your top takeaway from this chapter? Post what worked for you on social media with hashtag #Sell! or #DaleCarnegieTraining.

> *In a world of text messages, social media and emails, caring about and being able to relate well to others gives you the edge more than ever before.*
> —Dan Heffernan, chief sales officer, Dale Carnegie Training

3. VALUE
(You're Already Late to the Party)

I got in the Lyft at 2:52 p.m. near Providence, Rhode Island. My immediate thought was, *Can I trust this guy?* The driver, Joe, was a strong, heavy guy with sleeves rolled up, exposing his fully tattooed arms. He wore a beanie-style winter hat and was playing Mötley Crüe loud in his high-mileage sedan.

"Long drive ahead of you, eh?" I said.

"What do you mean? Where are we going?"

"Logan Airport."

"What? Oh, man, I didn't realize that when I accepted the ride." He paused to consider, then continued firmly, "But don't worry, I'll get you there."

I've heard stories of many taxis and ride-sharing drivers declining a passenger when they find out the ride will take them over an hour away from their hometown. My driver, Joe, would have to fight terrible Boston rush-hour traffic trying to get home after dropping me off, almost surely without any passenger to compensate him for the long drive back.

That was only part of the story, though. Not only did we have a long way to go, I was cutting it close, trying to catch an earlier flight. I'd been traveling a lot lately for work, and there was a slim chance that if I got on that flight, I could have make it home in time to put my kids to bed.

From the backseat, I disappeared into work phone calls, one of which was to the airline. I could get on the earlier flight, but I estimated I'd have to get to the airport no later than 4:00 and make it to the gate fast. The ETA on Joe's phone on the dashboard said 4:06.

"If we can get there by 4:00, I might get home to Minnesota for my kids tonight. I'd appreciate anything you can do to get me there. Thank you for doing this, Joe," I pleaded from the backseat.

He nodded quietly.

As we got closer to Boston, I was no longer on the phone, so he started talking.

"I used to drive a truck in and out of Boston, but I haven't been up here for years. I got injured, so I couldn't keep driving. Some guys might sit on the couch collecting money from the government and drinking beer. I decided I'd keep doing whatever I could do. So now I do this driving, along with some local trailer driving for a guy in town. I'd rather not be in Boston traffic tonight, but you need to get to the airport and I said I'd get you there.

"You know, I love Minnesota. I lived there when my dad went through treatment for cancer at the

Mayo Clinic. The locals at the hotel, Jimmy John's, and the hospital were my only support. They were the nicest people and made such a difference when my dad finally died after three months. I'm going to get you to Minnesota to see your kids before they go to bed."

As he weaved and maneuvered as aggressively as he could through traffic, I watched the ETA on his phone move up and up, recalculating the drive time because traffic was increasing closer to the airport. But Joe kept at it. Studying the airport signs carefully, he found his way to the curbside drop-off. It was 4:03. He couldn't have safely done anything more than that.

"It was my pleasure to do this. Get home to Minnesota and see your kids."

Of course my gate was the furthest in the airport from security. I sprinted down the hallway, down and up escalators, and around corners. Just as they were about to close the boarding doors for my gate, I arrived. Heaving deep breaths, I got to my row as the woman in the aisle seat smiled, got up, and made room for me to settle.

Three hours later I was lying with my kids, kissing them to sleep.

What makes a guy like Joe willing to be inconvenienced? Here's a guy who has plenty of reasons to complain in life. But instead he chose to help. I imagine him sitting in bumper-to-bumper traffic on 93 South after dropping me off, with Mötley Crüe blasting, thinking, "Even though this was inconvenient, it feels really good to help."

Perhaps the path to joy is through inconvenience. It causes us to get outside ourselves and affirm our value.

I was grateful for Joe. Not just that he got me to the airport quickly, but because he inspired me to be inconvenienced for other people.

It might be simply allowing someone to get in front of you in line. Maybe it's helping someone at work. Or perhaps it's a willingness to do something extra for the benefit of others.

Like Joe, don't just do it begrudgingly. Do it with commitment. Where can you inconvenience yourself for someone today?

This story was written by Matt Norman, managing partner of Dale Carnegie in Minnesota, Iowa, and Nebraska.* It's a powerful illustration of everything we have talked about so far—trust and credibility. But it's also a beautiful example of the third element in effective selling: *mutual understanding of value.*

You see, when Matt got into the Lyft, he developed a relationship with Joe. It wasn't a long-term relationship. We doubt they're sending each other holiday cards. But for the time that they were engaged in the business transaction, it was a relationship. And they both understood the value of the experience.

---

* Matt Norman, "How a Lyft Ride Reminded Me of the Importance of Helping Others," Matt Norman website, Feb. 4, 2019: https://www.mattnorman.com/importance-of-helping-others.

For Matt, he had to trust that Joe would get him to the airport on time. The value of Joe delivering him on time meant that he would be home in time to tuck his kids into bed.

What about Joe? Joe had to trust that driving Matt all that way would be valuable. Was he doing it just for the sale? In the hopes that a well-dressed man would leave him a big tip? Not likely. Joe defined the value of his work in terms that were beyond money. To him, it was a matter of integrity and commitment. "You need to get to the airport, and I said I'd get you there."

In this transaction, both Matt and Joe had a mutual understanding of the transaction's value, and it was based on respect. Matt respected Joe's work ethic and integrity. Joe respected the fact that Matt wanted to get home so he could tuck his kids into bed.

The Real Value of the Transaction

It seems like a straightforward question: when you buy something: what is the value of the transaction? You can look at your bank statement or PayPal account and see what you paid, right? That's the value of the transaction.

No. That's only the cost. As we saw with Matt and Joe, the value of the transaction goes far beyond the monetary exchange for a product or service. Even in the simplest sale, the money is the least important aspect of the transaction.

In the subtitle of this chapter, we said, "You're already late to the party," because by the time you get into the sales situation, your customer has already extensively researched your product or service. The global marketplace is so vast that for any item that a person might need or want, there are usually hundreds or thousands of options to choose from. Do you need ballpoint pens? Google brings back more than 22 million results for you to choose from in fifty-two seconds. Need a new car? You can order it online and have it delivered. Got a bad back? Search "chiropractor near me" and get 88 million results.

If you're going to compete in the global (or local) marketplace, you've got a lot of competition. In business, there are three main areas of competitive advantage: *price*, *quality*, and *convenience*. It used to be that you could compete in one or two of the three areas, but not in all three. In other words, you could have the lowest price, but the quality would suffer. Or you could offer convenience, but it would cost more. High quality often meant high prices.

But today, in the Age of Amazon and Time of Target with the Wonder of Walmart, you can get all three with a few taps on your phone. With few exceptions, your customers are able to get everything you offer cheaply, quickly, and with equivalent quality. Worse yet, they can also get a ton of information, so if you were thinking you'd be an information resource, you can think again.

So what's a salesperson to do? Remember Mike from chapter 1? He was the guy who had lost the sale before he'd even gotten back to his car. He was lamenting that he couldn't compete with the Amazons of the world.

Luckily, you now know something that Mike didn't, and that little secret is going to help you increase your earnings and success. You've learned that it's more important to be a trusted advisor to your customers than it is to have the lowest price.

Trust Me, I'm a Salesperson

What does it mean to be a trusted advisor? It means that you are considered a subject-matter expert in your industry and are the go-to guy or gal when your clients have a question or an issue.

Let's say you come out of the market, put your bags away, and get in the car, and it won't start. You could use your phone and search "my car won't start." Your results will give you lots of information on car batteries and starters. You might find diagrams of ignition systems. You'll probably get sponsored ads for mechanics and tow trucks. But you won't find information on what is wrong with *your* car.

So what are you going to do? You're not just going to flag down some random stranger unless you absolutely must. Most likely, you have a roadside assistance plan, and you'll call them. Why? Is it the cheapest option? Probably not. Is it the most convenient? Maybe, but maybe not. There isn't a huge quality difference between the various towing companies. No, you're going to call your roadside assistance company because you *trust them* to tell you what is wrong with your car and help you solve the problem of being stranded.

Mike from chapter 1 didn't understand that the only real way to compete in today's environment is to differentiate yourself by becoming a trusted advisor. We are rapidly approaching the time when robots take over the busywork jobs and artificial intelligence takes over the logic of inter-preting and learning from data. So, what does that leave for you, our dear member of the subtribe *Hominina*? It leaves your humanity.

As a human, you have the capacity to develop rela-tionships with other humans. You have likely heard the acronym "USP," or *unique selling proposition*. This term usually refers to what makes your company or its products uniquely valuable relative to other options in the market. Your own USP in the marketplace is your ability to feel, to get emotionally connected to your clients, and to *care.* No computer algorithm or search engine can ever compete with your humanity.

When you become a trusted advisor, it's like putting on a bulletproof vest that keeps you safe from the cross fire of your competition. There is only one you. You are not a com-modity that can be easily exchanged for another. You are the only one who can use your experience, your knowledge, your judgment, and your intuition to help your customers solve their most pressing problems. The more valuable you make yourself to your customers, the more often they will come back.

How might you become more like the salesperson who remembers someone's birthday? Or the Lyft driver who'll drive out of your way so your passenger can get home to his kids? Or the one who is the first call your customer makes when they need what you sell? Let's explore what it takes to become a trusted advisor, and use the time-tested Dale Carnegie principles and sales process—how we can discover the winning combination to sales success.

The Bottom Line for Chapter 3

- The value of the transaction goes far beyond its monetary value.
- The days where you could compete on price, quality, or convenience are gone.
- By the time you get into the sales situation, your customers already know about your product.
- The way to compete in today's environment is to become a trusted advisor to your customers or clients.
- The value of your product or service increases a hundredfold when you've earned your customer's trust.

What did you try from this chapter that worked for you? Post it on social media!

Part Two

The Dale Carnegie Sales Process

4. THE RELATIONSHIP COMES FIRST

At Dale Carnegie Training, we believe that relationships are at the heart of all sales. After all, it was our founder who wrote *How to Win Friends and Influence People*.

As we've said, you have to be in the relationship before you can influence the sale. You're not forming the relationship for the sole purpose of making money. Pallavi Jha, managing partner of Dale Carnegie in India, talks about how the traditional model of sales doesn't work very well there. She says, "India is a country where relationships play a big role. In business you create relationships to leverage something. Having the right connections opens doors faster. You meet someone, start building the relationship, and hope it pays off. But you're really only expanding the relationship you already have."

At this point you might be thinking, "I already have a ton of relationships. You should see my Facebook and

LinkedIn pages. I'm very popular. But I need to know how to take those relationships and leverage them into sales." "Likes" don't buy dog food.

How to Get into a Business Relationship

If you already know how to get into business relationships, then great. You already have done what we've been recommending. Your "number" is getting bigger all the time. But are they the right kinds of relationships? Are they the people who are actually in the market for what you sell? If you're an event planner, for example, are most of your contacts other event planners? It's fine to have a solid network of peers, but you need a list of prospective customers. Despite what those spam emails tell you, buying a list is not the best or most efficient way to build your database.

Get out and go to where your customers are. That might be a leads group, the Chamber of Commerce, a trade show. Wherever your people congregate, go there and talk to them. It's the timeless way of doing business, and is just as relevant as it was in 1937. Talk to folks. Get them to like you. Find out what they need, and then give it to them. It's that simple. We've got a bunch of suggestions for you in the next chapter, but the idea of a systemized pre-approach to meeting and developing relationships with the right people is the first step in our process.

The Dale Carnegie Sales Process

Congratulations. You took our advice and you're out networking and meeting people and you've got a stack of cards or e-cards and have entered them into your CRM. Time to blend up a margarita and start waiting for the sales to start pouring in, right?

You wish.

Now you need a systematic approach to transforming those relationships into actual sales. While you need to be in the relationship before you can start selling, you do want to start selling. Whether you're in Alaska or New Zealand, the purpose of sales is to, well, sell stuff.

In our training programs, we teach a five-step process for navigating the psychology of a business relationship that leads to sales. In the next few chapters, we'll go into detail about each step in the process, but for now here's an overview. Take a look at the graphic on page 69. You'll notice what is in the circle in the middle of the graphic. It's the *customer relationship*, where your goal is to transform your golden status as trusted advisor into something you can buy groceries with. Here are the steps in the cycle:

Connect. Find prospective customers and ways to meet and connect with them.

Collaborate. Work together with your buyer to find out what the issues are and how you can best help. This is where the "trusted advisor" part happens.

Create. Create a mutual understanding of value. Remember, the value is more than the money part of the transaction. This is where you find out what they really want.

Confirm. Make sure you've really heard what they've said. The old adage that "you have two ears and one mouth for a reason" really applies here.

Commit. Finally, get them to commit to the sale. (Hint: it's not just asking them to buy your stuff.)

To help you understand how these steps are connected, we're going to put a graphic at the beginning of each of the next five chapters.

Are you excited? Sure you are. Let's connect, in the next chapter.

The Bottom Line for Chapter 4

- Relationship-based selling means that you establish trust first, and then find out what they need.
- This means you're going to have to network. Sorry, but it's true. Becoming a trusted advisor is much easier when you actually know the person in real life.
- After you're in the relationship, you need a systematic approach to leverage it into sales. Hey, we just happen to have a systematic approach!
- The purpose of sales is to meet the needs of the buyer. The Dale Carnegie sales process is used around the world to successfully meet the needs of buyers.

5. CONNECT

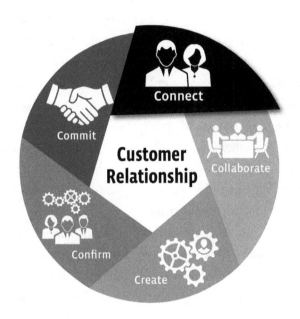

Herb Escher, Dale Carnegie's managing partner in Rochester, New York, demonstrates how he uses the Carnegie principles to connect. Assess your connection skills. Would you have started this sales call the way Herb did?

I received a call from a potential client. Sharon was reaching out to me because she and her boss saw an opportunity to develop their leaders. She conveyed a clear passion for her people over the phone. I had not heard of her company before. I knew the first thing I had to do was get in front of them so I could understand why they see it as so important to develop their leaders. After I got off the phone, I did a Google and LinkedIn search of the company. I saw it was a heavy-machinery manufacturing company, and it was a family business. I drove to the appointment in the suburbs of Buffalo, found their building, and noticed they had no signage in front. As I walked, their waiting area showed pictures of their employees and corresponding years of service. Most of them had been there for ten, thirty, and even forty years. The receptionist told me she had been working for the company for twenty-eight years and that she had made lifelong friends there.

Sharon took me to the conference room, and Brad, the COO, was sitting there. She introduced Brad, stating that he was the third generation to run the company. Brad got up, shook my hand, and welcomed me. I sat down, looked at both of them, and said, "Wow! I was in your waiting room, and I was blown away by seeing the picture of all your employees and the years that they have worked here. Your receptionist told me she's been here for twenty-eight years and has made lifelong friends."

I asked them what they were doing to have such a strong culture. They both looked at me and smiled with pride. Sharon thanked me for noticing and told me she also had lifelong friends working there. Brad told me they like to build a culture with a foundation of respect. He started telling me about the history of the company. We started talking about leadership, and about why Brad wanted to see his leaders become stronger. As he was talking, I took notes on my iPad. When he finished, I asked him, "Before I tell you how we can help, may I ask for a tour?" Brad responded, "I'll take you myself! But before we go on a tour, tell me more about Dale Carnegie." So I explained what we do, but made sure I explained it in the context of what he was striving to accomplish. He and Sharon were both nodding their heads and smiling.

Brad started the tour in his break room, which, he said, they keep stocked with food for the team so they can eat anytime. He then took me to the shop floor, showing me the machinery they make and how they make it. He showed me the welding of the machinery, explaining the welding process. I asked him if keeping welders was difficult because of the shortage of welders. He explained that it is critical to have enough welders: if they don't, they can't deliver their products. I asked how many welders, and he said 120. I responded with a question: "So having leaders engaging them could give you a real competitive advantage?"

He said, "Yes!"

I asked him if the union has ever tried approaching their people.

"Yes, all the time! Buffalo is a union town."

"So it's essential for us to have your leaders building trust?"

"Yes, very important." I then told him about our engagement research and how it ties into what they were looking to accomplish. He then showed me their world-class workout facility and how wellness is vital to them.

I sat down again with Brad and Sharon. I asked them both, "What's your time line?" They told me, "ASAP," so I walked them through a program that could help them accomplish their goals and told them a ballpark investment figure. They told me they wanted to get started in April. We came up with a project calendar, envisioning when we would start. I told them I'd put a proposal together for their review so we could move forward.

I sent them an email thanking them for their time, and how I completed the first draft of the proposal. They emailed me back telling me we are a great fit for them, but they'd like it scaled back. I made some modifications, and we agreed to move forward together.

The first thing I did was connect. Most salespeople are eager to ask what they are doing wrong, but I wanted to focus on who they are and honor that. That is why preapproach is not just from the Internet. Don't sit down when someone tells you to sit down in the waiting room. Engage with people to get to know what they like about working there. Your job is to make a friend and build trust. Then look on the walls for what someone would be proud of. This could be patents, announcements, articles, or awards. When you build that trust, people will be open to tell you the truth about what's going on, because you've taken down the wall of "I'm here to sell you something."

Connecting to build trust is your foundation, so what's the value of understanding a complete sales process? The sales process is really just gaining insight into how customers buy. Once you know how customers buy, you can make it easy for both of you. Here's some practical advice from Rick Gallegos, Dale Carnegie's managing partner in Tampa, Florida, who has consistently earned global awards and recognition for both market penetration and effective sales training.

When I started my career fresh out of college selling Dale Carnegie Training, I was very enthusiastic and superfriendly. I thought that these two key traits would power me right to the top of the sales team of ten people! It had certainly worked before in college. Boy, was I sorely wrong! After six months, once my training salary ended and I started on commission, I was $3,000 behind on my draw because of low sales, and it felt like I was million dollars behind. Everything I was trying was not working. The joke in the office was, "Maybe he should take the sales course; it probably can't hurt!" Well, I did, and it was life-changing for me. I learned that sales is a *process* that occurs and requires preparation and execution. Once I learned the system, it made everything so much easier. I had a playbook to follow, and follow it I did. I went from last place on our team to second, and after a year had the highest sales on the team consistently. I was promoted to team leader, sales manager, and vice president of sales. I always think about these early years in my career when I am facilitating a sales program and share this story very often to let everyone know the value of what they will be learning.

Now let's get into the process. It's time to go out there and find those prospective customers. Whether you've been in sales for thirty years or thirty minutes, one thing remains the same: you can't succeed with just one client, no matter how big. You need the next one and the one after that. You need to leverage one buyer into the next prospect—or even many prospects. Prospecting is essential. Over the course of your career, you will sometimes need to replace customers, and you will definitely need to find new ones.

The Difference Between a Prospect and a Lead

Let's make sure we understand the terms we're using. In sales terminology, a *prospect* is different from a *lead*. A prospect is someone who may buy from you. It's a flesh-and-blood person. A prospect can sign a check. A lead is *not* a flesh-and-blood person. Usually it exists in the form of information, which sometimes is a bread-crumb trail to a real prospect. For example, a lead may be the name, phone number, or email address of someone who visited your website and downloaded information. A lead gives access to a prospect, who, if all goes well, may be a decision maker.

Prospecting Methods

In the old days of the Gold Rush, prospectors would stick a pan in the sand of a river and scoop some up. They would filter out the parts they didn't want and try to find nuggets of gold that they could sell for cash.

That's in essence what we're doing in sales. We go out to the river of people in the world and we look for the people who are candidates for your product and service.

What prospecting methods can you use to find that river of people? We can hear what you're thinking. You're probably thinking, "Please don't tell me to cold-call. I hate cold-calling. Cold-calling is dead, right? Some sales gurus say it's dead. Don't make me cold-call."

Is Cold-Calling Dead?

Trust us. We don't like the kind of cold-calling you're thinking of either. The kind where it's dinnertime and your phone rings and it's someone on the other line going, "How would you like to save 30 percent on your mortgage?" No one likes it. We don't like making those calls, and we don't like getting them either.

But cold-calling is not dead. It works. If it didn't, no one would do it. It's one of those time-tested methods, like separating your dark laundry from your lights, that you might try to skip for a while, but you'll soon realize that it is a good idea. Cold-calling is a necessary step, like washing your white clothes in hot water.

Cool Tips for Cold-Calling

John Torre* offers some good suggestions for making cold-calling easier.

> The first thing to do—before picking up the phone to call a prospect cold—is your homework. Take a minute or two to visit the prospect's website. Familiarize yourself with their company, what they do, what role they have at their company. This process can go a long way during the actual phone call itself because it adds a more personalized touch to the call and shows the prospect that you are genuinely interested in them.
>
> Also work on your introduction. Bland introductions tend to be a one-way ticket to getting hung up on in the first thirty seconds. The impact your greeting leaves on a prospect will determine how long they permit you to engage them. The trick is to strike a balance between formality and casual charm. Your greeting should also contain your name and your company name, as well as a little about your company. Avoid coming off as vague and elusive just to get an appointment.

---

* John Torre, "How to Improve Your Cold-Calling Skills," Dale Carnegie Training of Michigan website, July 22, 2013: http://www.dalecarnegiewaymi.com/2013/07/22/how-to-improve-your-cold-calling-skills.

When you finally speak with someone, don't skirt around the issue—just cut to the chase. Think of this as a declaration of your reason for calling. One of the more effective ways to state your purpose is to phrase it in the form of a question. Opening with a question sparks the potential for conversation, which is what most prospects would rather have than fielding an overly rehearsed sales call.

Perhaps the biggest area where salespeople drop the ball is in their follow-up. Every phone call requires some kind of follow-up, especially if you've left a voicemail. A quick email after leaving a voicemail is one of the best ways to follow up on a phone call, especially if you provide useful information. After that, put some time between your next phone contact. A minimum of three days should go by before you reach out to a prospect again. Anything less may leave them feeling pressured or hounded.

Despite the ease and convenience of mass email marketing, the sales game is still all about salespeople's conversational skills. People want to buy from people they like and trust. That is why it is so important for salespeople to put a sincere effort into their sales calls. So observe and heed the advice listed above. By doing so, you will be well on your way to more successful cold-calling.

Networking, Revisited

Networking is another one of the prospecting methods that strikes fear in the heart of pretty much everyone at first. It can be nerve-racking to walk into a room of people you don't already know. (There's a reason they usually have a bar set up at the entrance. Everyone else is nervous too!)

Let's say you're new to the game, or you sense that your networking skills might need some touching up. We've all seen that guy in the nineties power suit working the room and talking to someone just long enough to hand out his card and move on to the next victim. You don't want to be that guy. Here are some tips on how to network with ease. (Trust us, this can be a lot of fun!)

First, to take the fear out of a networking event and give yourself confidence, just reflect on these five simple, profound, and time-tested Dale Carnegie human-relations principles:

- Principle 4. Become genuinely interested in other people.
- Principle 6. Remember that a person's name is to that person the sweetest and most important sound in any language.
- Principle 7. Be a good listener. Encourage others to talk about themselves.
- Principle 8. Talk in terms of the other person's interest.
- Principle 9. Make the other person feel important—and do it sincerely.

Now here's a practical approach for applying those principles in a business context.

Networking Interview

When networking, set a goal to spend 80% of your time listening and 20% talking. Use this Networking Interview as a guide. As Mr. Carnegie wrote, "Become genuinely interested in the other person. Be a good listener and encourage others to talk about themselves."

Imagery	Memory Cue
	Start with an introduction and a handshake. *"Nice to meet you, I'm ..."*
	Smile. Make a positive observation. Such as: *"Wasn't the speaker fascinating?"*
	Learn about his or her job. *"What organization do you represent?"* *"What is your role?"*
	Find out if they came for a specific purpose. *"What brought you here?"*
	Uncover the issues or changes the individual or organization is experiencing. *"What are some of the challenges or changes affecting you and your organization?"*
	Share a success story, if appropriate.
	Find out how you can be of assistance to them. *"What can I do for you?"*
	To end the conversation graciously, simply say, *"It was a pleasure meeting you, (name). Perhaps we can have coffee in the near future."* Or *"It was great to meet you, (name). I'll connect with you on LinkedIn tomorrow!"*

Jonathan Vehar, vice president of products for Dale Carnegie Training, describes how a huge client came from a conversation about dogs that happened at a convention focused on creative thinking. "One of the partner's wives was in attendance, and during a break she struck up a conversation with another person at the conference who had dog treats on his 'creative' name tag. Since she loved dogs, it was an easy conversation to start. While engaging the other person and finding out more about him, his dogs, his family, and his job, she discovered that he was in need of the services of our company. This led to an introduction to the partner, our company, the dog owner's company, and it turned into a long-term relationship, with his company being our largest client for several years." This illustrates the power of principle 8: "Talk in terms of the other person's interests."

No conversation on this topic would be complete without touching on social-media networking. This is best used *combined with* in-person networking or, if you sell online, at least setting up online video meetings. It's the way to keep the conversation going.

"No, that's not true," you may say. "I've gotten a ton of subscribers to my newsletters and new contacts from social media."

We don't doubt it. But how is it going in converting them to sales if you never meet them in person or online via video? You might have some success, yes. But if you think about it, people buy from folks they trust. And if you have the chance to buy from "that guy who writes the newsletter from Widgets R Us" or "Scott, the guy whose kid goes to the same college as mine, and who sells widgets," who gets the sale?

We've said it before, and we're going to say it again so many times that it might as well be a drinking game. *The way to keep sales from being sleazy is to focus on building authentic relationships in which you can become a trusted advisor.* Is it possible to do this through online-only networking? Yes. But it's much, much harder than if you put on your big-girl (or big-boy) shoes and head out the door.

This advice is coming to you from the people who literally wrote the book on influence. Trust us, it works.

Referrals

While we are on the subject of things that strike fear in the hearts of salespeople but are also really effective, let's talk about asking for referrals. In our audio program *Sell Like a Pro,* we go into a lot of detail about how to get referrals. It really is one of the core skills in sales, but it can cause a lot of unnecessary anxiety.

For a lot of us, asking for referrals feels a lot like asking a guy if you can date his sister (or brother, as the case may be). It can be awkward. "Uh, hey. Yeah. So, do you think you might know of anyone else who might be in the market for ?"

It doesn't have to be like that! If you think of it differently, it really becomes a natural extension of the conversation. By far the most powerful weapon you can have when approaching a new prospect is a referral—an endorsement from someone the prospect knows and respects. The referral can come from a personal friend, a business colleague, or both. For sales pros, getting referrals is a top priority at all times.

If you made the sale, then you know you've found one person who values your solution. If Joe the Lyft driver had said to Matt, "If you know anyone else who needs a ride to the airport, let me know, man," what do you think Matt would have said? "Sir, I am deeply offended that you would ask such a question. I do not want my friends or family getting to the airport on time. How dare you even ask?" Of course not. When you are the trusted advisor, other people *want* to share you with others. It makes them look good!

What if you haven't made the sale? Maybe the timing is not right, or the person really isn't ever going to buy your product. Is asking for a referral such a big deal? No. Not then either.

Have you ever been shopping and saw something that wasn't right for you, but would be perfect for someone you know? Maybe it's a shirt that is the wrong size or style for you, but you look at it and think, "Jerry would love this!"

That's the same mind-set you use in asking for referrals. You're looking to find the Jerry that would love what you sell. You're not asking for the phone number of someone's grandmother so that you can call and bug her at dinner. You're simply asking another person if they know of anyone who has the problem that you solve. But you *do* have to ask for it. And you have to ask in the correct way.

Getting Referrals:
The Wrong Way and the Right Way

As salespeople, we've all fallen into traps in asking for referrals that can lead us to the wrong person or to no referral at all. For example, asking "Is there anyone else who might be interested?" is a mistake. It's a closed question, to which the answer can simply be no. When we ask for "anyone," it doesn't really help the buyer to think about specific people we can contact. So be more specific. Ask for a specific "who," not a general and vague "anybody" or "somebody."

So ask about someone else whom the customer knows and who might have a similar problem that your product or service solves. The more specific we can be, the greater our chances of getting a referral. "Whom do you know who is having product-reliability problems?" "Who is having problems with computer support?" "Whom do you know who wants to get the same results?" Those are the kind of sharply focused questions that have the best chance of getting good referrals.

Go to conferences and exchange business cards. Talk to people who are in positions of public contact, like reception staff and personal assistants. After any business-related conversation, always ask for referrals. And always say thank you.

Don't Waste a Referral

A referral is going to open a door for you. Don't waste it through lack of sufficient knowledge. Take the necessary time to research the individual, the department, the company, and the problem that needs to be addressed. Once you're sure you've learned as much as you can, you're ready to make initial contact with the prospect. Almost always this will be done with a phone call. If you have an email address for the referral, it won't hurt to send a message informing the person that you'll be getting in touch. But unless you get a reply, you should assume that your email either was not received or was not read.

Three Elements of the Referral Call

Remember the credibility statement we did earlier? This is a great place to use it. When you make the first call, your first few words are the most important, so you want to get them right. Follow this template: Always state your name first, even if the person you're talking with will have no idea who you are. Then ask to speak with your referral, and mention the name and affiliation of the person who gave you the contact.

It might go something like this: "Good morning. This is Steve Parker. I'm calling Janet Sloan, referred by Brian Hunt at *The Wall Street Journal*." Notice three elements: (1) your name; (2) the name of the person you want to contact; (3) the identity of the person who gave you the referral.

If you're calling a corporate office, sometimes you'll be asked the reason for your call. So once again mention the name of the person who gave you the referral, and add some information about how the referral came about. You might say, "Brian suggested I get in touch regarding computer support."

Don't feel you have to go into any more detail than that. Less is more. And just use the first name of the person who referred you. One important key to successful phone communication is to be very respectful but also informal.

Usually the person on the other end of the line will mirror your approach. If you're tense, they'll be tense. If you're calm, low-key, and confident, you'll get the same positive energy back.

It may take a few tries to connect with your referral. Keep trying, but don't keep trying forever. If it's obvious you're not going to get through, just shift your attention to another referral.

If and when you do get the referral on the line, once again introduce yourself by name. Then mention the person who referred you, along with a brief reason for your call. "Brian Hunt at *The Wall Street Journal* suggested I call you about computer support."

If you get a neutral or positive response, go one step further. "I was able to help Brian with a computer-support program, and he thought you might be in the market for something similar. Is that correct?"

If the person agrees with what you've said, continue with a normal sales call. If the person disagrees, wonder aloud why you were referred to him or her. You might say, "Maybe I haven't got the right information. I wonder why Brian gave me your name."

Sometimes this will open the door to further discussion. Other times it will just give you an opportunity to sign off from a referral who is clearly not interested. Occasionally it will even lead to another referral. In any case, always keep the person who referred you in the loop about the outcome. He or she will appreciate knowing what happened and may give you more referrals as a result.

Voicemail

One more thing about the telephone before we leave this topic: what about voicemail? Whether they admit it or not, most salespeople look at voicemail as a dead end. They say to themselves, "Oh well, I'll leave a message; maybe I'll get a call back." They don't really believe that, but some of us are so relieved not to have to talk with someone that we leave a message anyway. That's how we avoid dealing with a potentially negative response.

This can lead to some dangerous ways of thinking. By the time the day is over, we might feel good because we've made a lot of calls and left a lot of messages, but our real productivity has been minimal. Over time, that can take its toll.

Voicemail becomes the starting point for locating the person you're trying to contact. It's the starting point because you're not going to let it be the ending point. This is another area where the all-important credibility statement can come in handy.

Instead, hit the "0" button and do your best to get a live person on the phone. When you do get connected to someone, here's how the dialogue might go: "Hi, could you help me out for a second? I'm trying to get hold of Mr. X, and I got his voicemail. Would you happen to know if he's at lunch, or on vacation, or in a meeting?"

Notice you aren't just asking to find Mr. X. You're also providing possible solutions for finding him. This helps the phone receptionist feel as if he or she is part of the problem-solving process.

The receptionist is likely to offer one of two responses. The first is, "Yes, he's in a meeting (or at lunch, or on vacation), and I'm not sure when he'll be back at his desk."

This answer has just given you a lot more information than you would have had if you had just left a voicemail. Now you know your contact's whereabouts in real time, and you can call back at a better time.

The second possible response is, "No, I really don't know where he is." In this case, you reply, "That's not a problem. Would you happen to know anyone whose desk or office is near him or who works in his area who might know where he is?" Again, you're offering another option. Sometimes the receptionist will then transfer you to a colleague of your contact who can help you.

But the receptionist might also reply, "No, I don't know anyone in his area." You then say, "Would you happen to have a paging system or his cell-phone number by any chance?"

If the receptionist can't help you at that point either, just say, "Thank you very much. I really appreciate your help." Then hang up and call back another time.

You're still much better off than if you'd just left a voicemail and let it go at that. You've been much more proactive and resilient. And more often than you might expect, you'll get through to your prospect simply because you took a few extra steps.

The most important elements for finding new prospects—whether by referrals or otherwise—are optimism and resilience. Develop an inner certainty that you will find new buyers even if you face some rejection in the process. And as Dale Carnegie always emphasized, a genuine interest in people is essential.

We can see this in our own relationships. When we have a conversation with someone, we can quickly pick up on whether that person really likes us or is indifferent to us—and we are much more likely to do business with those who like us.

Sometimes you'll speak with a prospect who initially seems uninterested in you. When that happens, you're much more likely to convert them when you express interest in them—in their needs and how your product or service can meet those needs.

The Small Paper Clip
That Turned into a Huge Sale

Jonathan Vehar shares a great story that illustrates how important it is to find a connection, even when you're not intending to connect the way you do.

In response to a request for information that was handled by an assistant, we sent the prospective client an informational package that contained $45 worth of materials: a copy of our book, a very expensive brochure, a demo video, other sales materials, and a business card, all held together by a colorful paper clip that just happened to be in our company colors.

I followed up with a phone call a week later, and the prospect remembered me by saying, "Oh yes! You're the one that sent me that wonderful"—at this point my mind was wondering if she was going to be excited about our book or our expensive and clever brochure, or maybe the video?—"paper clip! I've never seen one like that before!"

While I was briefly deflated because this was what caught her attention, I rallied, and we had a very nice conversation about color and how it adds to the work space. By the end of the conversation, she had turned into a client that I would work with for years. Look for opportunities to make a connection, no matter how small or unexpected.

Other Ways to Connect

So far we've talked about cold-calling, networking, and referrals. What other prospecting methods can you use to fill your pipeline and connect with prospects?

Competitor websites. Is it ethical to go over to a competitor's website and mine their success stories and customer profiles? Of course. It's a free world, and if you are able to become the trusted advisor to someone who has already been in the market for your product or service, there's nothing wrong with it at all. Remember, all we are looking to do is build a relationship with someone and see where it leads. Use the guidelines appropriate for your culture or industry, but never feel bad about approaching someone to have a business relationship with you.

Blogging. Do you have a personal website or blog? If you do have a personal site, do you update it at least once a day—and preferably more often than that? Do you make signed contributions in the comments or forum sections of sites belonging to others? Are you taking part in the online social-networking revolution that is totally changing the way people meet and interact?

All these questions are related, but the most important one is the first one. If you do have a personal website or blog, chances are you're actively participating in the electronic universe in other ways as well.

Your purpose in online prospecting is to be seen by the largest possible number of people. That purpose is best served when you seem conversational, informal, and energetic without being overwhelming. There are dozens of ways of doing this. Keep updating your site's information. Don't let anything get stale. Don't let people come back to your site and see the same thing they saw the last time.

Email Prospecting

Want to be more effective and efficient with e-mail? The next time you're about to send an email to a potential customer, answer yes or no to the following questions:

- Are you sending the email in order to avoid making a call?
- Is email your choice because it lets you avoid the rejection that you experience when you make cold calls?
- Do you wait for return emails before moving the process forward with a call?
- Are you using email to efficiently qualify your prospects and decide whom to call?

You can see the defensive psychology that underlies these questions. Anticipating rejection makes us turn to email to generate new prospect relationships. We think it will hurt less to get a computerized negative reply than to actually hear the word *no*. On the other hand, we can use email marketing tools to call people who open, respond to, or forward emails, which is just plain smart.

Another negative motivation for email reliance is getting blocked by gatekeepers or voicemail when making phone calls. When salespeople don't know how to get through those barriers, they think, "Forget it—it's not worth the aggravation and energy. I'll just email instead."

As we've mentioned, the credibility statement can really help to build trust, and using it in email is no exception. Most introductory emails contain a traditional three-part sales pitch—the introduction, the mini-presentation about the product or service being offered, and the request for a response. This instantly tells the recipients that the email's objective is to attain your goals, not theirs.

Email Prospecting Pitfalls

With all this in mind, if you're still using email to connect with new prospects, watch out for these pitfalls:

1. Avoid obvious sales pitches. Make your message about issues and problems that you believe your prospects are having, but don't say anything to indicate that you're assuming that both of you are a match.

2. Remove your company name from the subject line. Don't create the impression that you can't wait to give a presentation about your products and services. Your subject line should refer to concerns that you can help the buyer solve. It should be about them, not you.

3. Stop teaching your prospects how to hide behind email. When you rely on email, it's easy for buyers to avoid you by not responding. They also get used to never picking up the phone and having a conversation with you. They may be afraid to show any interest, because they think you'll try to close them. This creates sales pressure, which is the basis of all selling woes.

   Next, avoid using *I* at the start of your message. Starting an email with *I* gives the impression that you care mainly about selling your product. You need to open a conversation, so use collaborative rather than individual phrasings. If you can use the language of a natural conversation, your buyer won't stereotype your message as a spam solicitation.

Asking for the Appointment

Now that you've found someone you like, it's time to ask for the date. No, you're not bringing a red rose, but in order to have a sales call, you have to have an appointment.

In fact, Neville De Lucia of Dale Carnegie Training in South Africa, likens sales to dating. He says, "You wouldn't just walk up to an attractive stranger and ask them out on a date. You have to develop a strategy to do that. You go to the places they are, show that you're interested in them as a person and the things that they are interested in. *Then* you can ask them out.

"Selling is about activity. If times are tough, be more active. If it used to take ten meetings to make a sale, and now it takes twenty meetings to make the sale, your activity ratio has to change. Improve your skills, identify your customers, and put it into your sales process."

By the time you get to the stage of being ready to ask for the appointment, the process is pretty straightforward. To ask for the appointment, develop your own *appointment power phrase*. It looks like this:

1. Reason for contacting, tied to key issues.
2. Brief statement on how you are solving problems like theirs.
3. Ask for appointment or ask for permission to ask questions.

A simple piece of advice from De Lucia is to make sure that people put the appointment into their calendar; this way they are less likely to cancel. If someone says, "Sure, come on by the office," ask them, "When is convenient for you?" Then follow it up with a calendar invitation.

"Sales is the most valuable skill in the world," De Lucia adds.

The Preapproach

The last topic in this chapter is what we like to call the *pre-approach*. It's research that you do before you walk into the meeting so that you can frame the conversation effectively. Here are some things you want to check out before you open that door.

• Key information about the people, company, industry, etc.
• Specific call objectives
• Issues that represent selling opportunities
• Common ground or contacts that might be helpful
• Resources you can offer that add insight or value

The Bottom Line for Chapter 5

- A *prospect* is a person who might buy from you; a *lead* is a piece of information, often generated from buyer research on your company, that gets you to the prospect.
- Cold-calling is not dead, but it's not what you think it is either.
- Networking is a great way to begin an authentic relationship.
- Social-media networking is best used *before or after* in-person networking.
- Referrals are the single best source of prospects if we approach them correctly.
- Be careful that you're not using email to avoid the other ways of prospecting.
- Use preapproach research to identify some talking points before the appointment.
- The secret to networking is simple: become genuinely interested in other people.

6. COLLABORATE

"Come on in, Edward. Have a seat."

Edward Perlman was happy to have this appointment with Stan Brown, VP of operations for one of the largest supermarket chains in the country. Edward's company produced point-of-sale (POS) technology for stores, and he was here to talk about updating the company's registers.

"Thank you for seeing me," Edward said, pulling out a chair. After some initial chitchat, they got down to business. "So tell me about some of the problems you're facing with your POS systems."

"Our biggest problem is that our cashiers are too slow. During peak hours, we have to have a full staff and open every line. This results in increased hourly expenses, because we have to pay for more employees per shift. If they were more efficient, we wouldn't need to have as much manpower per hour.

"We need two things. We need newer machines so that we can speed up the transactions. And we need to train the cashiers to talk less. Talking to each other and all the chatting with the customers is slowing things down."

Now at this point, Edward could launch into his sales pitch. After all, the prospect very clearly stated what he wanted, right?

Wrong. Stan gave what he *thinks* is the solution to his problem. The fact is, he isn't necessarily even correct about what the real problem is, let alone the solution. He only knows the solutions he was able to find when researching Edward's company. If Edward is able to ask additional questions to get additional information, he can then figure out what Stan's real issue is.

In our experience, the problem that the client initially describes is rarely what they need to solve. By assuming that what the client is asking for is what they really want, we miss the opportunity to elevate the conversation beyond a mere transaction and take it into a longer-term relationship where we focus on delivering what is necessary for them to succeed.

The Power of Questions

Dan Heffernan says, "If you had to pick just one Dale Carnegie principle and master it to be great at sales, and successful in life, to me it's this one: try honestly to see things from the other person's point of view. I've seen salespeople with great empathy get stunning results because they truly care. For example, this year we have a twenty-six-year-old salesperson breaking into Fortune 50 tech companies almost purely by empathizing with her customers. I've seen her get four times the average sales volume of her peers with decades of experience. Most of the other reps knew our products better and had more well-rounded skills. But she is so deep in her ability to listen and empathize that it has been a more powerful factor in getting results for her customers. At the heart of this principle, you need to ask effective questions to understand the world from your customer's point of view so you can help them. Sometimes it's natural for you, but if it's not, that's OK; we have a roadmap."

The Questioning Model

Dale Carnegie Training has developed what we call the Questioning Model to help you discover what your customers really need. It's a series of questions that guide the buyer along the path of discovery. You start at where they are now and then ask questions that reveal where they want to be.

This process of gathering information should be conversational and capture the information required to present your solution in a compelling way. Make your solution unique for each customer by using the information you learn from this model. Here's a visual representation, along with descriptions and samples for each stage.

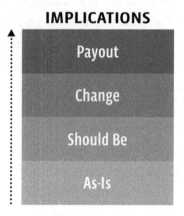

IMPLICATIONS

Payout

Change

Should Be

As-Is

As-Is Questions

These assess the customer's current situation. They give you a picture of key issues, such as product specifications, influential decision makers, and challenges that you may be able to address with your solution. Use the information you gleaned from preapproach research to ask informed questions. Examples:

• How has (use preapproach info) impacted your operation?

• Who are your current providers? How did you select them?

• Why did you start to (use preapproach info)?
• What would you change about your current providers?

Should-Be Questions

Should-be questions help you discover the customer's vision regarding your solution at optimum performance. These questions focus on how the customer's situation would be different if you helped solve his or her problems. Examples:
• How will those impact you?
• Where would you like to be six months from today?

Change Questions

Change questions identify factors that prevent the customer from achieving the should-be. These questions determine what needs to change before the should-be is attained. Examples:
• What changes would you like to see?
• What other factors are important to you?

Payout Questions

Payout questions clarify how the customer and/or the organization benefits from the solution. Responses to these questions allow you to understand and appeal to the motivational reasons for buying.

Asking payout questions separates the most successful salespeople from everyone else. Most salespeople are intimidated by asking this question, either because they think they have enough information already, or more likely, they're afraid it may come across as a challenge. I've noticed that more than any other question type, this gets customers to pause and reflect before they answer you. That's good. You're becoming a trusted advisor. As long as you've done your job building trust using foundational Dale Carnegie principles, then use principle 21 and "throw down a challenge." Examples:

- If you're able to (should-be), what impact will that have on your company/team?
- What could happen when you're able to (should-be)?
- What would you do with the additional time/revenue/ resources saved?
- How will you measure the success of this initiative one year from now?

Risk versus Reward

What is the cost of inaction if your customer does nothing? That can be an incredibly compelling buying question.

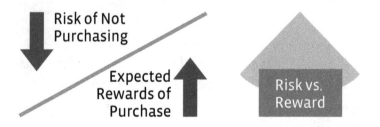

One key element that you want your clients to think about is "What is the cost of doing nothing?"

Jonathan tells this story from a previous organization, "because our service [new product development] was focused on helping clients grow their business, we found that this question about the cost of doing nothing would make them pause and think about the downside of not investing in their future success. We wanted to shift the conversation from, 'Wow, that's a lot of money!' to 'Yikes, if we don't spend this money, we could be in trouble.'"

The Power of the Pause

There are cultural variations, but almost everyone gets uncomfortable after a certain amount of silence. But savvy salespeople understand the power of the pause. Very often, the first answer someone gives to a question is the answer they think they should give; it's the one that first comes to mind. If you pause, however, and resist the urge to jump in to fill the silence, often the next thing that is said is deeper and truer than the first, reaction answer. Similarly, there are key words and phrases that cause people to shut down in conversation. Matt Norman (the guy from the Lyft) elaborates.*

> Sometimes a simple word or phrase is all it takes to send people fighting or hiding. Are you careful to notice what words and phrases might do this?
>
> Here are some examples:
>
> **The let-down:** My uncle taught me to avoid using the word *unfortunately*, as in "I'd love to be able to help with that. Unfortunately, I don't have time." It's a let-down word. Notice how often customer-service people use this word. "Mr. Norman, your business is

---

* Matt Norman, "The Power of the Pause," Matt Norman website, Aug. 14, 2018: https://www.mattnorman.com/pause.

very important to us. Unfortunately, we have a policy that doesn't allow us to do that." Ugh. Now it's time for fight or flight.

The tee-up: The VP of sales at a company I worked for would rail on people for using the phrase "to be honest," as in "To be honest, I don't think we should do this." "Are you normally not honest?" he would ask, pointing out that the qualifier made it sound like the person usually *didn't* give it to him straight. That made me wonder how often people are more guarded when I tee up an opinion with that qualifier.

The shut-down: *No. But. However.* A colleague of mine once quipped that "but" is really an acronym for *Before the Ultimate Truth*, as in, "I hear what you're saying, but I disagree." It shuts people down. Puts them on the offensive. Guards go up.

Life is filled with enough polarization and conflict. Let's not perpetuate it with words and phrases that let down, confuse, or shut down interactions.

What can you say instead of these words and phrases? How about *nothing*? Just removing them and replacing them with a relaxed pause is often enough to keep everyone on the same page.

Another option is to say *yes and*. Perhaps you've heard this suggestion, popularized in improv comedy. Few activities require as much cooperation as improv comedy. It doesn't work if people get let down, thrown off, or shut down. It needs to keep building.

The same applies to *any* interaction. In meetings, email, and personal dialogue, we need to use words that keep people open to listening and working together.

The Questioning Model in the Real World

John Rodgers, managing partner, Dale Carnegie Training for Pittsburgh and Cleveland, writes:

> Dave, a top window and door salesperson, was practicing asking question types to improve his skills during a group coaching session. To facilitate the process, we agreed he would be selling to a homeowner (my role) who had just purchased a rental and potentially needed to replace the windows.
>
> We worked our way through refining and improving as-is questions, should-be questions, change, and finally payout questions. Everyone participated, Dave especially took some great notes, then everyone took off to reengage in their work.
>
> Later that afternoon Dave received a call from a gentleman who said he had just bought a rental property. He and his wife were considering buying new windows, and could Dave answer a few questions? Dave immediately thought, "This is obviously John Rodgers calling to test me from this morning sessions."
>
> Being a good sport, he rolled his eyes and decided to play along. After all, right on his desk were

his refined notes and improved questions from the morning session , so he grabbed them with a grin and immediately transitioned from the customer's questions to gaining permission to ask a few questions to conserve his time. He was on a roll (after all I did not stop and correct him), so with great confidence he launched into his questions. Then the gentleman on the phone asked if he and his wife could come right down to the showroom to see what he was talking about. Well, of course, Dave said again rolling his eyes thinking, "John is really taking this a bit far"—after all he had plenty of work to get done this afternoon—"but I'll go along with it."

Dave was stunned when a customer (who was not me) showed up at his office and said, "We just had a conversation an hour ago about windows"; could Dave show him what seemed to be a perfect fit for his rental properties? Dave jumped to his feet, and within twenty minutes the customer placed a $28,000 order. Dave was now a real champion for the process.

In this chapter, we've talked about ways for you to *collaborate* with your customer or prospect and really get down to what their key issues are. In the next chapter we'll learn how to *create* solutions to the issues that we've uncovered.

The Bottom Line for Chapter 6

- The questions we ask determine the answers we get. Practice asking questions that will lead to better information and position you as a trusted advisor.
- As-is questions give you additional information about the current status of the customer's situation.
- Should-be questions tell you how the customer thinks things should be. This identifies the buyer's gap.
- Change questions involve the things that have been preventing the customer from getting to how things should be. They're what needs to change before they can get to should-be.
- Payout questions help you both to understand what the benefit of making the change will be.
- Risk versus reward compares the cost of inaction with the reward of action.
- Try honestly to see things from the other person's point of view.
- Post your top takeaway on social media to improve your learning retention.

Talk to someone about themselves
and they'll listen for hours.
—DALE CARNEGIE

7. CREATE

Before we launch into the *create* stage of our process, here are the Dale Carnegie principles you can use to improve your ability to collaborate with and create compelling solutions for your customers.

Win People to Your Way of Thinking

13. Begin in a friendly way.
14. Get the other person saying, "Yes, yes" immediately.

15. Let the other person do a great deal of the talking.
16. Let the other person feel that the idea is his or hers.
17. Try honestly to see things from the other person's point of view.
18. Be sympathetic to the other person's ideas and desires.
19. Appeal to the nobler motives.
20. Dramatize your ideas.
21. Throw down a challenge.

Let's revisit Edward and Stan from the last chapter. We last left our dear friends in a sales meeting, where Stan was saying the cashiers talked too much and were inefficient, causing him to have to pay for more staff during peak hours.

Through Stan's answers to the questions asked with the Questioning Model, Edward was able to discover that a certain percentage of customers value talking to the cashier. It's a major part of the shopping experience for them. Imagine an elderly woman whose sole activity on a given day is to get to the market to buy a few items. She lives alone and doesn't have many people to talk with in the course of her week. If she gets to the market, and the cashier is trained not to talk to her but to get her through the line as fast as possible, she's likely to start shopping somewhere else. The need that the market is filling is less about the food the woman is buying and is more about the shopping experience. So speeding customers like her through is not always the best solution.

Edward realizes that if Stan is concerned about staffing additional cashiers, he could put in some self-checkout machines for customers who just want to get in and out. Also purchasing some new point-of-sale (POS) systems would make it easier for customers who are in line but also want to have interaction with the cashiers.

These are the solutions that Edward believes will work for Stan, and now he has to present them as a trusted advisor. Again, the goal is not to push the self-checkout machines or POS systems. It's about being Stan's trusted advisor and helping him to find out what he is really selling, what is the actual problem, and finding out whether or not the solution Edward comes up with has value to Stan.

Six Key Steps to Delivering the Solution

Greg Story, author of *Japan Sales Mastery*, outlines six key steps for delivering the solution to the customer:

1. Give the key fact or figure.
2. Build the bridge.
3. Introduce the benefit.
4. Apply the benefit.
5. Supply evidence.
6. Test commitment.

Let's take a closer look at each of them.

Give the key fact or figure.

The first thing you do in making your proposed solution is to raise a key fact or feature about it. This must be specific, true, provable, and highly relevant to what the buyer actually wants and needs.

Build the bridge.

Before linking the facts to the corresponding benefit, we need to set up a bridge to the new subject of the
conversation—the benefits. "Let me tell you why _____
is important."

Introduce the benefit.

Only now can you introduce the benefit of your solution.
It's been said a million times before, but it's worth saying
again: *features* and *benefits* are not the same thing. It doesn't
matter how many bells and whistles your widget has. It
doesn't! What matters is what those bells and whistles can
DO for the buyer. Those are the features.

Does this mean you don't tell them about the features?
Of course not. The features lead to the benefits. Your job
is to summarize them and then connect the features to the
benefits.

Apply the benefit.

Now it's time to describe how the benefit is applied. It's all
fine and good to say that your solution provides a benefit.
But how will your buyer apply it to improve their situation?
Help them visualize what success will look like by painting a word picture that connects them emotionally to what
your solution will feel like.

No doubt you read principle 3: *Arouse in the other person an eager want*. Not as easy as it sounds, right? Here's
the secret: paint a word picture. People buy for a variety
of reasons, but emotional factors make them *want to buy*.
Use word pictures to summarize the value of your solution

and activate their emotions, creating a sense of urgency and overcoming procrastination.

Remind yourself of what your customers want (primary interest) and why they want it (individual motive). Then do these four things:

1. Remind your customer that he or she lacks the benefit your solution provides. Get his or her agreement.
2. Remind your customer that your solution will help him or her realize that benefit.
3. Paint a word picture of your customer using your solution, enjoying it, and benefitting from it.
4. Ask for a commitment.

Your word picture should:
- Show the customer benefiting from your solution.
- Appeal to his or her emotions.
- Be clear and concise.
- Be in the present tense.
- Be believable and realistic.
- Activate the senses—sight, sound, touch, taste, and smell.
- Appeal to his or her individual motive.

Supply evidence.
Now it's time to put your money where your mouth is. You've painted this amazing word picture of how great things can be if the buyer just adopts your solution. But as everyone who has ever watched a political debate can attest, promises mean nothing. "Where's the proof?" This is the time to share examples, facts, demonstrations, stories, analogies, that show that what you've been saying is true.

Test commitment.

Having gotten this far, the buyer is likely to be smiling and nodding yes. But, as we've learned, in some cultures smiling and nodding and even saying yes doesn't mean they are ready to buy. It can mean, "Yes, I understand what you are saying." So you need to test out how eager the buyer is to purchase what you're selling. It can be something as simple as:

"How does that look for you?" (for visual types) "How does this sound so far?" (for auditory types) "What do you think about this?" (for logical types)

"How do you feel about what you're hearing?" or "Would you like to try it?" (for kinesthetic types)

Edward, Stan, and the Six Steps

So how would our friend Edward use the six steps with Stan? Here they are again.

1. Give the key fact or figure.
2. Build the bridge.
3. Introduce the benefit.
4. Apply the benefit.
5. Supply evidence.
6. Test commitment.

"Stan, what we found is that 90 percent of shoppers aged eighteen to thirty-nine found self-service checkouts easy to use, but only 50 percent of those over sixty said the same. From what you've told me, 45 percent of your shoppers are senior citizens. (1) "What this means for you (2) is that self-service checkouts will appeal to the majority of your customers, but not all.

"The benefit of having a combination of both self-service checkout and updated POS systems is that you can appeal to both age ranges. (3) Imagine it's Friday at 5:30 pm. Prime rush hour for your markets. You have four self-checkout terminals, and your younger customers are speeding through. Then in your cashiered aisles, the automated POS system, like the one I showed you, makes your lines go faster. The customers who want to talk to a cashier for their social needs can, and the ones that don't can use self-checkout. (4) Use of self-checkout kiosks is predicted to double in the next few years. (5) Does what I'm saying make sense?" (6)

You can see that when Edward presented his solution to Stan this way, it naturally progressed from what he identified were Stan's actual challenges to how his proposed solution will meet them.

The next likely step is for Stan to start raising objections or concerns, and we'll get into that in the next chapter.

The Power of Stories in Sales

But first let's talk a little bit about the power of stories in sales. So far in this chapter, we've suggested several times for communicating specific value propositions to the buyer. Facts and benefits are one way to provide value, but many times sales professionals rely too heavily on these. As Dale Carnegie said, "Merely stating a truth isn't enough. The truth has to be made vivid, interesting, and dramatic."

A great way to bring to life facts, benefits, and ultimately your product's solutions is to tell a story. It is much easier for your customer to retain benefits and solutions when you center them around a story.

In research done for his book *The Hypnotic Brain: Hypnotherapy and Social Communication,* Peter Brown demonstrated that stories synchronize the teller's and the listener's brain waves and enable similar areas of their brains to engage.

Stories don't feel persuasive or manipulative. And they allow you to address the competition without trash-talking them.

In an informal survey, 100 percent of the people asked said that stories were important in the sales situation, 85 percent of them said they use stories, but in reality only 20 percent did. Why is this? Why don't more people use stories?

"I don't have any stories prepared."

"I'm a bad storyteller."

"I can never remember them."

"I don't have any stories."

"No one wants to take the time to hear my stories."

In our Dale Carnegie sales training programs, we teach a quick and easy way to develop and deliver a story with confidence and ease. It's called the Magic Formula: Incident + Action + Benefit = Magic Formula.

> ## Incident + Action + Benefit = Magic Formula
>
> • Describe the customer's situation before implementing your solution.
>
> • Explain how your solution was implemented.
>
> • Emphasize how your solution created value for the customer.

When you use the Magic Formula, developing a story is almost effortless!

Ten Keys to Effective Sales Storytelling

1. Determine the prospect's backstory.
2. Develop several stories to have on hand.
3. Ask yourself what you want the story to do.
4. Keep it targeted to the listener and his or her backstory.
5. Determine the point you want to make.
6. Tell a complete story that leads to your point.
7. Stay attuned to the customer's reaction to your story.
8. Practice your story before the sales situation.
9. Be very specific about how you can help solve the problem.
10. Be authentic.

Let's talk a little more about each one.

Determine the prospect's backstory.

Now you might be thinking, "I did this when I did my pre-approach, and then asked them all those questions. I know this guy so well, I bet he friend-requests me."

The backstory is not the same thing as the reason the buyer agreed to have you come in for the sales call. The reason you're there is that the client has a problem to solve. The backstory is the reason they are in the position they're in. The buyer's backstory is just that—a *back story*. It's everything in their past that led them to this point. Their attitudes, how they feel about the world, and how they fit into it. Think of them as a character in a novel or a movie. What happened in their lives to get them to this point in the story? If we look back at Matt and Joe in chapter 3, Joe's backstory was everything that led to him becoming a Lyft driver. If you were selling something to Joe, that's what you'd need to determine in order to share a story that's relevant to him. It's not his current motivation, it's everything that led up to it.

Develop several stories to have on hand.

We've all had it happen. You're sitting there with someone and you think, "Oh, I should tell her about that time when I had a customer who had the exact same problem." But you don't have the story prepared and can't remember all the details specifically. How long ago was it? What was the client's last name again? If you want to use storytelling in sales (and, trust us, you do), you need to think of specific stories that fit certain needs. Sit down and write them out.

Ask yourself what you want the story to do.

This goes with the previous section. Each story you tell should be for a specific purpose. Maybe you want to illustrate risk versus reward. Or use your story as evidence and social proof that your solution works. Whatever your reason, make sure you're clear on it before you open your mouth.

Keep it targeted to the listener and his or her backstory.

Another key to remember is to stay focused on your listener. It's easy for stories to wander from one to the next, and the next thing you know your listener is sitting there wondering, "What does this have to do with me? I don't even own an alpaca."

Determine the point you want to make.

This is similar, but slightly different from what you want the story to do. The purpose of the story is to lead to one clear point: "Buying our product can solve XYZ." Or "Our customer service is available 24/7."

Tell a complete story that leads to your point.

Have you ever been at a family dinner, and there's Uncle Bob, who tells a random, meandering story that never seems to end? Don't be that guy. A story should have a beginning, a middle, and an end. The beginning is the setup. "One time, we had a client in Ferndale and they needed to get to the next biggest town over, Eureka, to pick up their delivery." The middle is the action of the story. "The problem was, they had too much rain, and the one bridge in and out of town flooded. No one was going in or out except service personnel. Well, our customer-service rep put all of the stuff in the trunk of his car and drove down to the bridge. He talked to the repair guys, who said that the bridge would be open later that afternoon. So he worked from his car for the rest of the day, and when the bridge opened, he was the first person to cross over into town."

The end of the story is where you connect it back to the listener: "So you don't have to worry at all about not getting the items you need. We are so committed to our customers that we are willing to go the extra mile. Literally." Beginning, middle, and end. Boom.

Here's how you want to structure your beginning, middle, and end.

- We worked with . . .
- They were aiming to . . .
- As a result, they were able to . . .

Stay attuned to the customer's reaction to your story.
This is incredibly important. Stay engaged with your listener. Not everyone wants to hear a story. Some kinds of decision makers just want the bottom line. If they start showing signs of boredom (looking at their phone or out a window, or fidgeting in their seats), it's time to end the story and move on.

Practice your story before the sales situation.
"So, one time, I think it was about a year ago. No, two years ago. No, wait. I had my new car, so it had to have

been last year. Anyway, so last year we had this big contract with ExxonMobil. Wait, I mean a large energy company. Ha ha ha, you didn't hear that. So anyway, we had this contract, but the senior vice president was really arrogant. He went to Harvard, so what do you expect? I hope you didn't go to Harvard, ha ha ha. Anyway, so this arrogant guy . . ."

At what point in this story did the narrator lose you? Probably early on. In order to tell a compelling story, you need to practice! Do you think that actors and comedians just walk out on stage and tell a story or a joke in front of an audience for the first time? No! They practice their technique beforehand. Don't worry about getting it down word for word, but get across your main ideas. Memorizing is not necessary. But if you think of your story in pictures, you'll remember it just fine.

Be very specific about how you can help solve the problem.
It's important to be very specific about how you can solve the problem. The story is just an interesting vehicle to deliver your promise. In the end, though, it's important to really be clear and specific about the fact that you *can* solve the customer's problem.

Be authentic.
This almost goes without saying, but we are going to say it anyway: Be real. Be you. Don't try to sound like Morgan Freeman telling a story. Just tell the story in a genuine way that is authentic to you and the way you speak.

Speaking Tips

Even the best story can fall flat if it isn't said right. Things like the syllables you stress, the pitch and tone of your voice, how fast or slowly you say something can all affect how information is received. Here are some tips that you can use when practicing your stories.

Stress

Practice saying the following sentences aloud, stressing the italicized words. Note the different meanings conveyed.

1. *We* need to grow our business.
2. We need to *grow* our business.

By emphasizing *we*, the speaker is indicating that she or her team needs to take responsibility for growing the business. In the same next sentence, with a different word emphasized, the meaning changes. The speaker is indicating that many things may be going right with the business, but people need to take more responsibility for growth.

Pitch

Varying the pitch in your voice can convey meaning as well. For example, say the following sentence using a high-pitched voice (as you would talk to a baby or a pet), your normal pitch, and a low pitch.

"Come here."

When said in a high-pitched voice, "Come here" sounds like a request. When said in a lower-pitched voice, it sounds like a command or even a threat.

Speed

Many different effects can be achieved by varying the speed of your words. Say "thirty million dollars" very fast, as if that were a trivial sum of money.

Then say, "Thirrrrttttyyyy millllionnnn dollllarrrsss," extending every syllable to the maximum. Now it really seems like a lot of money. By increasing the time you took to say it, it's almost as if you've increased the amount itself. Yet the actual words you've spoken are just the same.

Don't Be Uncle Bob

Here are some things to avoid in storytelling:
- Lecturing
- Jargon
- Failing to watch how the story is being received
- Making it too long or too short
- Failing to link the story to the prospect's backstory
- Telling your favorite story just because it's your favorite

In this chapter, we've covered a lot of tips and techniques for creating and then communicating your suggested solution to your prospects. In the next chapter, we'll get into listening to their concerns and doubts and then addressing them.

The Bottom Line for Chapter 7

- There are six key steps to delivering the solutions to the customer. They are:
  1. Give the key fact or figure.
  2. Build the bridge.
  3. Introduce the benefit.
  4. Apply the benefit.
  5. Supply evidence.
  6. Test commitment.

- Telling engaging stories is a great way to communicate the value of your solution to the buyer.
- Great stories don't just happen. They are created.
- By telling a story that features your client, you're painting a word picture that arouses an eager want, appealing not just to logic but emotion.

8. CONFIRM

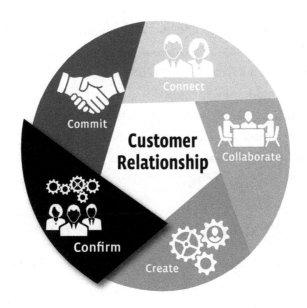

Nine times out of ten, an argument ends with each of the contestants more firmly convinced than ever that he is absolutely right.

You can't win an argument. You can't because if you lose it, you lose it, and if you win it, you lose it. Why? Well, suppose you triumph over the other man and shoot his argument full of holes? Then what? You will feel fine. But what about him? You have made

him feel inferior. You have hurt his pride. He will
resent your triumph. And—

"A man convinced against his will

"Is of the same opinion still."

—*How to Win Friends and Influence People*

Edward and Stan are still in their meeting. Stan has listened to what Edward had to say and heard the solution
Edward presented, so he should be ready and willing to just
sign on the dotted line, right?

Not likely. What's more probable is that Stan is going
to have some concerns and objections. The challenge for
Edward (and all salespeople, really) is to actually listen to
what the buyer has to say.

What Kind of Listener Are You?

In our book *Listen!* we describe the seven types of listeners
identified by Dale Carnegie Training.

• Preoccupieds
• Out-to-lunchers
• Interrupters
• Whatevers
• Combatives
• Analysts
• Engagers

The first six types are less effective than the seventh. Here
is an in-depth description of each of the types.

Preoccupieds

These people come across as rushed and are constantly looking around or doing something else. Also known as multitaskers, these people cannot sit still and listen.

Out-to-Lunchers

These people are physically there for you, yet mentally they are not. You can tell this by the blank look on their faces. They are either daydreaming or thinking about something else entirely.

Interrupters

Interrupters are ready to chime in at any given time. They are perched and ready for a break to complete your sentence for you. They are not listening to you. They are focused on trying to guess what you will say and what they want to say.

Whatevers

These people remain aloof and show little emotion when listening. They do not seem to care about anything you have to say.

Combatives

Hostile and rude, the combative listener isn't listening for understanding. He or she is listening to get ammunition to use against you. These people are armed and ready for war. They enjoy disagreeing and blaming others.

Analysts

These people are constantly in the role of counselor or therapist, and they are ready to provide you with unsolicited answers. They think they are great listeners and love to help. They are constantly in an analyze-what-you-are-saying-and-fix-it mode.

Engagers

These are the consciously aware listeners. They listen with their eyes, ears, and hearts and try to put themselves in the speaker's shoes. This is listening at the highest level. Their listening skills encourage you to continue talking and give you the opportunity to discover your own solutions and let your ideas unfold.

As you were reading this, you probably thought of people you know who fall into each of the categories. In fact, your buyers will often fall into them. You can tell if someone is really listening to you or not. And if your buyer isn't, then you need to know it to be able to turn the sale around.

Listening Principles

When you meet a potential customer, you should do more listening than talking. Show that you want to build a relationship, not just make another sale. Here are some tips for being an excellent, engaged listener.

1. Maintain eye contact with the person talking.
2. Be sensitive to what is *not* being said. Observe body language for incongruent messages.

3. Practice patience. Do not interrupt, finish the speaker's sentence, or change the subject.

4. Listen empathetically, and listen to understand. Act as if there will be a quiz at the end.

5. Clarify any uncertainties after he or she has spoken. Make sure you understood what was said by rephrasing what you heard.

6. Don't jump to conclusions or make assumptions. Keep an open and accepting attitude.

7. Practice pure listening. Remove all distractions.

8. Turn off your mind and be with the speaker. Try to see things from his or her perspective.

Listening proactively allows you to ask good questions and hear what is really being said. Do you usually listen at the highest level?

Be a Mirror

When you feel you've really listened to what buyers are telling you, you can prove it by reflecting back what you've heard. This doesn't mean parroting back the same words. It means using your own words to rephrase what's been said. When you paraphrase what you've heard, you demonstrate that you've listened to the buyer and have also taken the time to think about what he or she has said. This requires significant effort. When you make that effort, customers will see it and appreciate it.

We Told You There Would Be a Quiz

In the following scenario, imagine that your buyer is communicating to you.

"I don't know. I just wish that there was some way to make this whole process easier. I mean, first I have to power down the computer and reboot it, and if that doesn't work, it's a twenty-minute call to technical support. Half the time I get some outsourced person I can't even understand. The whole thing is really frustrating."

Now practice reflecting back what they said, using different words. Say or write out what you would say to demonstrate listening in a genuine desire to understand.

Stan's Concerns

As expected, Stan has some concerns that he shares with Edward.

"OK, so what I'm hearing is that you suggest that we upgrade our POS system in our lines, and install four to five self-checkout terminals in each of our 250 locations. There are a couple of problems with that.

"First, it's my understanding that self-checkout kiosks don't actually reduce the number of cashiers we have to have on staff at any given shift. And, second, those kiosks cost about $125,000 each. Why on earth would I spend millions of dollars to install kiosks when it's not even going to solve my problem? Not to mention the fact that I'd have to deal with increased theft."

It can be a challenge to really listen to objections. Most salespeople face the same handful of objections, and we tend to hear them all the time. We generally think we know what the buyer is going to say, and we often know how we will respond. This creates a tendency to jump in to respond halfway through. But this is an important time to slow down the sales process, listen for understanding, and see objections from the buyer's point of view. When the client gives an objection, it can be perceived in four ways:

• What they say
• What we hear
• What we interpret it to mean
• What they really mean

It is critical that, before responding to the client's concern, both the salesperson and the client clearly understand what the concern really is. Be careful not to interpret the objection, because if your interpretation is incorrect, your response might be off target. Instead, repeat back what you've heard and then cushion it. A cushion is a statement that acknowledges that you've listened to the prospect, heard the objection, and recognized its importance. When a buyer states an objection, your first action should be to cushion the objection. A cushion does not agree or disagree with or answer the objection.

Examples of Cushions

Objection: Your price is considerably higher than I expected.
Cushion: I appreciate your concern about the investment.

Objection: I am happy with my current provider.
Cushion: I'm sure your current provider has been satisfactory.

Objection: My staff is happy with the process they are using now.
Cushion: Certainly you want to keep your staff happy.

Objection: I do not think we're ready to make a change at this time.
Cushion: I know you want to make the right decision at the right time.

Overcoming Objections

The cushion is always step one. Terry Siebert of Dale Carnegie Wisconsin has this to say about an entire process for handling objections:*

> Dealing with objections requires us to practice careful, sensitive listening skills along with positive, factual responses to customer concerns. Of course, as with any part of the sales process, it helps to have a strategy. And just like driving a car, this strategy becomes second nature if we understand it, practice it, and are committed to using it when objections occur. Here is a proven, five-step process that tends to

---

* Terry Siebert, "Responding (Not Reacting) to Objections, Part 1," Greater Madison In Business website, Sept. 15, 2011: https://www.ibmadison.com/Blogger/Leader-to-Leader/September-2011/Responding-not-reacting-to-objections-part-1-0.

get better results than the usual "blame-deny-justify" approach:

Step 1: Cushion.

Just as a real cushion makes you feel more comfortable when you're sitting on a hard surface, the same is applicable in the first step in dealing with an objection. When you hear the objection, the cushion, in its most basic form, empathizes with the customer. For example, "I understand how you might feel that way."

The cushion never agrees with the objection, which would validate it in the mind of the customer. The cushion also never disagrees with the objection, which would start a confrontational scenario. If more salespeople just responded with a cushion to the objections they hear, I am convinced that they would be building better relationships with their customers. Finally, once the cushion is stated, be careful not to follow it with a "but." It tends to take the conversation in a negative direction. Rather, use the word "and"—it keeps the discussion on an even plane.

Step 2: Clarify the Objection.

Once you have cushioned the objection, you then need to clarify exactly what is behind the customer's concern. Most sales folks have heard the price objection more than they would like. The danger is that they assume they understand where the customer is coming from. Is it the price, the terms, the financing, the upfront payment, or something else? A good question here is: "Help me understand exactly what is it about (the customer's concern) that would cause you to hesitate?" Also, don't be afraid to dig a bit deeper here—you want to make darn sure you will respond to the real objection. If you are comfortable that you have a good handle on the real objection, you are ready to move on to the next step.

Step 3: Cross-Check (Identify Hidden Objections).

In this step, you are trying to determine if there are any hidden objections that are not on the table. It is not uncommon for some buyers to hold back. A question that I often use in this step is: "In addition to your concern with (stated objection), is there anything else that would prevent you from going ahead with this proposal?" If I get a positive response, we get that issue on the table as well. If I get a negative response, my next statement would go something like this: "So if we can resolve that concern to your satisfaction, there is really nothing else that is stopping you from going ahead. Is that correct?" This line of questioning is 100 percent intended to get the real objection(s) on the table to be addressed, and the smokescreen objections off the table.

Step 4: Reply.

You will note that we are not responding to the objection until step 4. Many amateur salespeople start with this step by reacting to the initial objection.

Step 5: Trial Close (Evaluate the Customer's Position).
A trial close is a question that asks for an opinion, not for a buying decision. Use a nonthreatening question to test the customer's reaction to a specific aspect of the solution. The reaction to the trial-close question helps clarify the customer's position regarding acceptance of what was just presented.

- How does that look to you?
- Does this sound like what you're looking for?
- What are your thoughts about this now?

Objection Handling In Action

Arkansas Carnegie consultant Jessie Wilson had a three-year partnership with a financial-services firm that suddenly needed to restructure. For the first twenty minutes of her meeting with them, she built rapport and asked personal and professional questions. Her client then informed Jessie they were going to hold off on any business for that year. Jessie nodded and asked questions to understand the reasons for not wanting to move forward. She asked questions to turn the conversation toward the results the firm had generated from the three-year relationship. She told stories from successful people at the firm who had cited Carnegie training as making their success possible. She then mentioned the names of people at the firm who had requested additional services that year. Her client said, "Maybe I need to reconsider." After more conversation, instead of cancelling the contract, the firm plans to increase its investment by nearly 20 percent despite the financial tradeoffs involved.

If Jessie had not started reestablishing rapport and connection, the firm would likely have ended up discontinuing the contract. One sign of this reestablished rapport is that Jessie was asked to stick to thirty minutes, but after building rapport the buyer offered to spend a full hour. The same would not have been true if she had not had the confidence to ask more questions and explore the rationale for the potential decisions.

Evidence DEFEATS Doubts

As the graphic on the following page shows, you can powerfully counter objections using evidence. The acronym DEFEATS helps us remember how.

D = Demonstration
E = Example
F = Fact
E = Exhibit
A = Analogy
T = Testimonial
S = Statistics

Here are some ways Edward can use this idea with Stan.

Demonstration. He could demonstrate the new POS system so that Mark could see its efficiency.

Example. He could share a story of another grocery chain that was able to counter theft by having the security guard who had been standing outside move to near the kiosks.

D	**Demonstration** An illustration using a physical demonstration with a prop or the solution itself.	
E	**Example** A story about a satisfied customer.	
F	**Fact** Statement of truth that supports the point you're making.	
E	**Exhibit** Something physical that supports your solution.	
A	**Analogy** A comparison of your solution to something with which the person is already familiar.	
T	**Testimonial** An acknowledgment of your solution's capabilities from someone who has used it.	
S	**Statistic** Accurate and relevant number that supports your solution.	

Fact. He could share the fact that it doesn't really cost $125,000 to install a kiosk.

Exhibit. He could show video or images of a competitor and how they use the kiosks.

Analogy. He could share a story that shows how customer satisfaction leads to increased sales.

Testimonial. He could share testimonials of other grocery chains who have used his solutions and of how well they worked.

Statistics. He could share statistics that show that the return on investment for self-service kiosks is high.

We may think that we have done a terrific job of resolving the buyer's objection, but it is what the buyer feels that is important. Before moving ahead, let's take a moment to evaluate whether or not the buyer is ready to move forward toward a commitment.

Examples: "Does that make you feel more comfortable about the lease payments?" "How does that sound?" "Does that address your concern?"

Here's how it looks in practice.

Hesitation. "My team is happy with the process they're currently using."

Response:

1. **Cushion.** Use a neutral statement that neither agrees nor disagrees. "Sounds like there's some satisfaction with things as they are."

2. **Clarify.** Ask a nonthreatening question to clarify the hesitation. "Do you think they'd be willing to learn a new process that would . . . (major benefit)?"

3. **Cross-check.** Confirm that the specific hesitation is the only factor preventing the commitment. "In addition to this concern, is there anything else causing you to hesitate?"

4. **Reply.** Deny, admit, or reverse the hesitation. Deny: deny falsehoods or misinformation. Admit: admit current or past problems. Reverse: turn objections into reasons for buying. "The process is easy to learn, and we'll help your team every step of the way."

5. **Trial-close.** Ask a question to determine if the objection has been resolved. "Do you think your team would be OK with that?"

Putting the *Go* in Negotiation

No book on sales would be complete without a discussion of negotiation. As with many of the topics in this book, Dale Carnegie Training has an entire training program on negotiation skills. But let's touch on a few of the core concepts here.

John Torre of Dale Carnegie Training wrote this on the subject of negotiation, sharing six tips for effective negotiation:*

> Folks from New Jersey are natural negotiators. As kids we negotiated trading baseball cards. As teens we negotiated with our parents in the hope of using the family car. As adults we negotiate with everybody— from the guy behind the deli counter to the salesman we talk to at our favorite car dealership.
>
> It was all good practice for when we turned professional, because as managers, the ability to use win-win negotiation skills can make all the difference in negotiating success. Likewise, it can be essential when influencing coworkers and facilitating constructive, positive relationships. Here are six things that managers should think about when preparing for a negotiation.

---

* John Torre, "Six Tips for Effective Negotiations," Dale Carnegie Training of Central and Southern New Jersey website, Sept. 14, 2011: http://www.dalecarnegiewaynj .com/2011/07/14/6-tips-for-effective-negotiations.

Know what you want. As a manager, it's important to go into a negotiation knowing what you want
your end result to be. Make sure you put a lot of time
and thought into what you want and why you want
it. Remember that it is important for you to consider
what's in it for you financially, emotionally, intellec-
tually, and physically.

Know what your counterpart wants. Your
counterpart will also have an agenda when he or she
enters the negotiation. Make it a point to understand
beforehand what he or she wants the conclusion of
this negotiation to be. Understand the financial, emotional, intellectual, or physical resolution that he or
she is looking to walk away with.

Anticipate objections. The negotiation process is
not always easy. As a manager, you have to understand that you will meet some objections from your
employee or significant counterpart along the way.
You need to prepare yourself for this by doing your
due diligence prior to the negotiation.

Identify concessions. Determine your absolutely
nonnegotiable items and what you are willing to give
and take. You are certainly not going to walk away
from every negotiation with all of your needs satisfied. Negotiations are all about the give-and-take,
and as a manager you need to be prepared to meet
your employee halfway.

Determine your walk-away. Prior to the start of
negotiations, define the point at which there is no

need to proceed with the negotiation. This will be your single most important source of negotiating power, so once your walk-away point is met, you need to make sure you take action.

Practice with a partner. As is the case with any important presentation you have ever made, you always want to practice. You could be faced with a difficult discussion, and it is always best to make sure you rehearse possible outcomes. By practicing with someone else, you will build your confidence with the situation, and it will ultimately help the negotiation run as smoothly as possible.

Consider these six criteria prior to your next negotiation and—*fuggedaboutit!* You're bound to come out on top.

Negotiation Best Practices

- Listen carefully.
- See from the other person's perspective.
- Be confident.
- Be prepared.
- Don't be aggressive.
- Don't make it a formal process.
- Look for creative solutions.
- Understand what is important to the customer.
- Negotiate details before price.
- Recognize walk-away points.

Negotiations In Action!

A senior counsel for a Fortune 50 organization wanted help negotiating multi-million dollar past due collections. Seth Mohorn, managing partner of Dale Carnegie in Arkansas, describes how by fundamentally changing his approach to negotiations, this lawyer yielded millions for his organization. In the past, the lawyers would aggressively 'hammer' the former client or partner to get as much out of them as possible. The problem was they normally only received a fraction of what they were owed on these deals by the time it reached legal. He decided to change his approach after completing Dale Carnegie training and applying the first nine principles. He explicitly told his former partners he would like to change the way they work together. He began in a friendly way, built rapport and expressed a genuine interest in his former partners for about 30 minutes . His first attempt at the approach earned him a $2.8 million commitment to pay within 10 days on a past due amount that in the past would capture less than $1 million.

What You Charge Is What You're Worth

Finally, we need to talk about the number-one objection that salespeople hear time and time again. "It's too expensive."

Here's how Jonathan Vehar addresses the money question.

Giving something away for free makes clients think your offering is worthless. During twenty-five years of selling, I have encountered a number of clients who promise that if we do a job for them for little or no money, it will lead to lots of future business. During the early years of our consulting practice, we sometimes accepted this "opportunity," hoping that it would turn into something big. It never did. But the projects we did for full price usually turned into long-term engagements.

We realized that these clients saw the free or low-cost services as being worth nothing or very little. They were very difficult clients to work with, because they did not trust us or our service. What we have since learned is that there is a perception that what you charge is what you are worth. So if business is not going well, rather than reducing the price, consider increasing your price so that people see your service or product as being more valuable.

In this chapter, we talked quite a bit about how to effectively listen to the concerns and objections of your prospect. We also covered some basic negotiation tips, and how to look at the dreaded price objection. In the next chapter, we'll put together the final piece of the puzzle: how to close the sale.

Let the other person do
a great deal of the talking.
—DALE CARNEGIE, PRINCIPLE 15

The Bottom Line for Chapter 8

- There are seven types of listeners, but only the engaged listener is really hearing what the other person has to say.
- Most salespeople hear the same few objections repeatedly. Our temptation is to tune the buyer out, thinking we already know what they are going to say. Resist that temptation.
- Reflect back to the buyer what you've heard them say in order to confirm.
- Then cushion their objection, and use the D.E.F.E.A.T.S. model to counter the objections.
- If you intend to negotiate the terms of the sale, determine what you will and will not concede, and always try to come to a collaborative agreement.
- If you discount your product or service too much, it reduces the perceived value in the buyer's mind.
- Practice Dale Carnegie principles 1 through 21, and your customers will buy more from you.

9. COMMIT

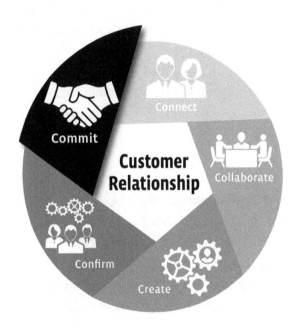

The first time it happened, someone was making a serious point about role clarity. "Each of us needs to be able to tell people exactly what we're working on," he said. Then someone else seized the opportunity for deprecating humor:

"Yeah, Chris can tell people that his job is to get projects over budget and behind schedule!"

"Ha ha!" Everyone erupted in laughter. So did Chris. But I studied his face and realized he was getting flush as his eyes looked down and his voice quickened. It took a while before he was really back in the meeting.

The second time it happened, another person in the meeting offered to help take care of a problem. "I'll help. My position has authority over that issue," she said with humility.

"Oh!" came a few shouts, "Alison's a big deal!" "No," she said quietly through nervous laughter.

"I was just saying that . . ." And she withdrew behind a smiling façade.

Matt Norman shared this story as part of a blog on how sometimes "joking humor" hurts.* How was Matt able to tell that there was dissonance between Chris and Alison's words and how they were really feeling? From the nonverbal signals they sent. Matt was a careful observer and was able to tell that they were pretending to be OK with what was going on in the meeting, even though they really weren't.

Buying Signals

In sales, you must be attentive to buying and warning signals. Watch for sudden changes in body language, facial expression, and vocal inflection. Be prepared to advance or step back, depending on what you observe.

In our book *Listen!,* we shared information on how to interpret body language. Of course, there are certain ele-

* Matt Norman, "When a Joke Humiliates: The Negative Impact of Offensive Humor," Matt Norman website, Nov. 15, 2019:https://www.mattnorman.com/offensive-humor.

ments of body language that can vary dramatically from culture to culture. It's not about having hard-and-fast rules, but more about looking for signals that convey comfort or discomfort. Is your buyer looking relaxed and at ease, or is he or she looking uncomfortable?

Ten Cardinal Rules of Observation

In his book *What Every Body Is Saying,* former FBI agent and body-language expert Joe Navarro gives ten cardinal rules of observation to use when you're listening to nonverbal communication.

1. You have to be a competent observer. This means you have to look around and observe the world around you constantly.
2. You have to observe all nonverbal communications in context. The context comes from the totality of what's going on in this person's life. (This is why understanding their backstory is so important.)
3. It's important to determine whether a behavior is coming from the brain or is cultural.
4. Are the behaviors unique to this individual? Most people have certain behaviors that they engage in repeatedly.
5. If you're looking at nonverbal communications that indicate thoughts, feelings, or intentions, it's best to look for clusters of behaviors rather than relying on one thing.
6. Ask yourself, "What is normal behavior for this person or in this situation?"

7. Also ask yourself, "What behaviors are a change from normal?"
8. Focus on primacy. Look for the most immediate expressions as being the most accurate, and use that information as you analyze nonverbal communication.
9. Make your observations nonintrusive.
10. Any time you see a behavior, if you're not sure what it means, always divide it up into one of two columns. Does it fit within comfort, or does it fit within discomfort? It's either going to be a comfort display or a discomfort display.

Body Talk

Because such a huge part of listening involves observing nonverbal signals, it's helpful to know what to notice. Again, it's important to take these items within the context of the ten cardinal rules.

According to Navarro, here are some interesting things to look for in order to tell when someone is comfortable or uncomfortable in their communication with you.

Feet

Our feet can indicate emotion. For example, when a person is standing and they plant one foot on their heel and they point that foot straight up into the air so the toes are straight up in the air, it's an indication of very positive emotions. If a person is tapping a foot, they are impatient or nervous.

The feet are also indicators of intention. Let's say you're talking to someone, and suddenly they start pointing one foot at the door. This is an extremely accurate intention cue of the message, "I've got to go."

Legs
When we cross our legs, this is usually a comfort display. We see it around people who genuinely like each other.

Arms
One of the truly powerful positions is arms akimbo. Most of the time, when you see someone standing with their hands on their hips, elbows out, legs slightly spread apart, this is a very territorial display. We see this when someone is in charge. It's a very commanding presence. It can also indicate a problem with the situation.

If you're trying to convey that you are interested and open, change the position of your hands so that your thumbs are facing the speaker.

Crossing the arms can have both positive and negative connotations. To determine which it is, you have to look at the grip. When people are talking to each other and their arms are crossed and they're gripping their arms very tightly, it usually indicates something very negative.

Otherwise, arm crossing isn't necessarily associated with something negative. One can have one's arms crossed, leaning back on a chair, and be very relaxed. When we are in a social setting where there are other people around us, we derive a certain amount of comfort putting our hands across our chest and so forth.

At times when we want to create a psychological barrier, we'll place an object like a pillow or a blanket or a coat over our arms or torso.

Hands

The hands are one of the best places to look for nonverbal messages. A firm handshake is a sign of dominance and aggression. A flaccid handshake is an indication of shyness. Women who have a strong handshake are indicating that they are open to new experiences. The same correlation isn't true for men. Superiors tend to have firmer handshakes than their subordinates, and friends exert equal pressure when shaking hands. Also, a quick handshake indicates a lack of interest or enthusiasm. A handshake that is slightly longer than normal is a sign of dominance.

We can talk about something expansive by using jazz hands—where we extend our fingers fully and they stretch. You'll note that politicians do this a lot.

Steepling is when we bring our fingertips together and don't allow our palms to touch, so that our fingers look like a church steeple. Steepling is in fact the most powerful behavior that we have to show confidence.

Shoulders

Imagine a teenager being asked, "Is your brother home from school yet?" She brings one shoulder up to the ear and says, "I don't know." But what if she is asked, "Is your brother home from school yet?" and both shoulders come up to the ears, she holds her palms up, and she says, "I don't know"? Which is more believable? The first (one shoulder only) indicates that she doesn't really want to talk about it. The second, with both shoulders and the hands, is more believable.

Neck

The neck is a place we tend to touch in order to soothe ourselves when we are under stress. Massaging the back of the neck while speaking is a classic indicator of discomfort. When women feel insecure, when they're distressed, when they're troubled or they feel threatened, they'll cover a little area called the suprasternal notch—the dimple in the neck between the two collarbones—with the tips of their fingers or with their hands.

Head

This is another area whereby you can observe if someone is listening to you or you can convey to someone that you're listening to them. You're talking to someone, and at some point in the conversation, your head begins to comfortably tilt as you're listening to them. If something is mentioned that you don't particularly care for, your head will immediately straighten up.

Forehead

The forehead is one of the easiest places on the body from which to determine anxiety. It presents us with a very accurate picture of a person's thoughts and feelings in real time. It can very clearly show us when there is stress, when there is comfort, when things are not going the right way, or when something is troubling us. If a person's eyebrows go up and his forehead indicates that he is anxious about what he is saying, that, combined with leaning forward and running his hands through his hair to self-soothe, can alert you that he is not comfortable with the conversation.

Eyes

Although most people think of blinking the eyes as merely a way of lubricating them, it's actually a very effective blocking mechanism. Most of the time, when we hear something we don't like, we will actually close our eyes. Sometimes it's just for a tenth of a second, sometimes it's for a little longer, yet it's a way the human brain has found to protect itself.

Many times when we hear bad news, or we are being told of something that stresses us, we'll find ourselves closing our eyes as we're processing the information. So if someone is listening to you and they close their eyes, it might not be that they aren't listening. It might be that they don't like what you're telling them.

Eyebrows

This is one of the classic comical gestures for indicating interest. A man looks at a woman, nods his head, and his eyebrows go up, as if to say, "How *you* doin'?" This is called the *eyebrow flash* and is a sign of comfort or interest.

Imagine meeting someone and, as you go to shake their hand, their eyes are just fixed. Then you meet another person and as you go to shake their hand, they look at you and they use the eyebrow flash. Which person is indicating more interest?

Mouth

When we have a true, sincere smile, the muscles around the eyes are engaged in the process. In a true smile, the corners of the mouth come up towards the eyes, and the eyes will reflect that, because the muscles of the eyes will be involved in that smile. (Unfortunately, this is where we get the crow's-feet effect.)

The false smile—the social smile—is the smile that moves the corners of the mouth towards the ears but does not involve the eyes. This is one way we can assess genuine emotions. The lips disappear, because the person is undergoing a high degree of stress. It has nothing to do with deception. It has nothing to do with truth or lying. Lip tension is mental tension. When the corners of the mouth also turn downward, then emotions are really low.

Biting the lip and cheek can have different connotations as well. This is why it's so important to keep these observations in context. For example, George W. Bush used to bite the inside of his cheek when he was nervous or anxious, and Bill Clinton had a tendency to bite his lower lip as a way of demonstrating his sincerity.

Chin

We've all seen the classic professor or therapist move—touching the chin or stroking a beard (real or imaginary). Chin touching is associated with pensiveness, with thinking, and with precision of ideas. We tend to show we're thinking of something by touching a narrow little area that is about two inches wide on the chin.

This gesture is to be differentiated from that of people who touch their face, especially around the jawline. We tend to pacify ourselves by touching our jaws. So when you see someone and they're touching their chin, they're thinking. If they're touching their jaw, that's more likely to be pacifying.

The jaw can also tell us about confidence or insecurity. When we're strong and confident, our jaw comes out. When we are weak and insecure, and when we lack confidence, we tuck our chin in.

Preening

We see it all over the animal kingdom: animals preen as an effort to make themselves look attractive to the opposite sex. Humans are animals too, yet instead of fluffing our feathers, we adjust our hair, glasses, or jewelry, or straighten our ties.

Preening in this manner sends a very powerful message to the other people who are in your presence. It subconsciously conveys to them, "You're important enough for me to spend this energy to put myself together to preen for you."

There are negative preening behaviors too. We see them in movies. A bad guy is trying to intimidate someone, and he starts picking lint off the other person's clothes or adjusts his glasses. It's a sign of disrespect, and when the other person allows it to continue, it's a strong statement of not having power in the situation.

Pacifying

We tend to think of pacifying as something that babies do to calm themselves down, such as sucking their thumb or twirling their hair. But pacifying behaviors continue on in adulthood as well. Here are some examples. When you see a person doing any of these things, it means that they are feeling anxious.

- Rubbing the forehead
- Pulling on hair
- Rubbing the nose
- Massaging the nose
- Pulling on the upper lip
- Stroking the chin
- Massaging the ears
- Pulling on the earlobes
- Twirling a pencil
- Mangling a paper clip
- Playing with a rubber band
- Rubbing the fingers
- Playing with jewelry (twisting a ring or pulling on a necklace)

SOFTEN

We've covered how you can use observations of nonverbal communication to listen to what a speaker is saying beyond words. You can also use these observations to let the other person know that you are listening to them. When listening, you can use nonverbal communication to SOFTEN the position of others:

S = Smile
O = Open posture
F = Forward lean
T = Touch
E = Eye contact
N = Nod

Red Light or Green Light?

Now that you've observed your buyer's nonverbal indicators and have used your communication skills to counter objections, you think you might just be ready to go in for the close. How can you be sure, though? A trial close!

Remember that a trial close is a question that asks for an opinion, not for a buying decision. Use a nonthreatening question to test the customer's reaction to a specific aspect of the solution. The reaction to the trial-close question helps clarify whether the customer has accepted what was just presented.

Examples:

• How does that look to you?
• Does this sound like what you're looking for?
• What are your thoughts about this now?

Let's say the buyer's nonverbal cues tell you that he or she isn't ready yet for the big trial close. Now it's time to swoop in with a word picture. Don't worry; you don't need to be Ernest Hemingway. Just follow a few guidelines and remind your buyer how wonderful life will be with the solution you're providing.

Word Pictures

While evidence and logic drive thinking about a decision, emotion usually powers it. You might think a POS system would be nice to have, but if you see your store traffic decreasing as customers hurry elsewhere, your fear motivates you to act.

Use word pictures to summarize the value of your solution and activate the emotions, creating a sense of urgency and overcoming procrastination. Many of our class members gain significant selling advantage by using strong word pictures. One member who sold pools would take small red flags and outline where the pool and spa were to be located in the backyard. She would bring the family to the middle of this area and have them imagine all of them swimming, playing volleyball, getting in the sun, and having a fabulous time together. More often than not this sealed the deal, because she understood the importance of emotion in the selling process.

Remind yourself of what your customers want and why they want it. Then do these four things:

1. Remind your customer that he or she lacks the benefit your solution provides. Get his or her agreement.
2. Remind your customer that your solution will help him or her realize that benefit.

3. Paint a word picture of your customer using your solution, enjoying it, and benefiting from it. Then, when the body language and verbal indicators tell you it's OK, you can—

4. Ask for a commitment.

Your word picture should:
• Show the customer benefiting from your solution.
• Appeal to his or her emotions.
• Be clear and concise.
• Be in the present tense.
• Be believable and realistic.
• Activate the senses—sight, sound, touch, taste, and smell.
• Appeal to his or her individual motive.

Emotion Trumps Logic

Dan Heffernan shares the following story from his experience in sales training:

> Tom Golisano is a billionaire who used his credit card to build his idea into a hugely successful payroll and HR outsourcing enterprise: Paychex. Our training team there was tasked with building a new online course to teach sales reps how to sell retirement plans using typical client scenarios.
>
> We were asked to present a demo of the course beta to Tom, who was then still the CEO. It was my first interaction with him, and I was anxious to know

his thoughts as he watched the laptop images we were projecting on the otherwise sterile conference-room wall.

We didn't have to wait long. Tom quickly asked to see how we intended to present the benefits of retirement plans to business owners. We displayed the part of the course that covered features and benefits, where he saw the phrase "maximize your retirement income." He then asked a question that my team later told me had them shaking in their boots.

"Where did you get the information you included in the course?" We told him we had interviewed top-performing sales reps and managers. He asked for names, which we provided. He nodded his approval as he heard names of people who had helped build the business. He pondered a moment. Then he asked another question, "Do you really think people buy retirement plans to maximize their retirement income?" At this point I had to take one for the team. "Yes, Tom, I do think so, but what are we missing here?" His response will stay with me always: "I think people invest in retirement plans so they can buy gifts for their grandchildren."

He had instantly humanized our environment and our purpose, and the room grew silent. "Makes sense, Tom, so you're saying we should appeal to emotion rather than logic here?" He answered with another question, "Don't you think that's how we make most of our buying decisions?"

I got to know quite a bit about Tom that day. I found him patient, considerate, thoughtful, and, as usual, demanding of a high standard. It was a fine example of the principled leadership that had contributed to his success.

Dale Carnegie said influence is about "arousing in the other person an eager want." If doing that well eludes you most of the time, remember to make an authentic appeal to emotion.

The Big Ask: Six Ways to Ask for the Sale

The moment is here. You've been preparing it for ever since you got the lead. It's time to ask for the commitment. Although this may be uncomfortable, if you have successfully built the relationship, asking for the purchase should be an easy step. Use a method that feels natural. Here are some to choose from.

The Direct Question
Often the best way to gain commitment is to ask for it. "Are you ready to go ahead with this decision now?" Or, "Based on our conversations do we have a basis for doing business?"

The Alternate-Choice Method
Ask the customer to select one of two options. "Would you like one from the standard stock or from our specialty line?"

The Minor-Point Method

If you've established trust and asked the right questions throughout the interview(s) with your customer, you can remove the anxiety buyers often feel when you ask for the sale by simply and confidently suggesting the next step. It might be to schedule something, to ask who should review a contract, or to describe options for your product or service.

The Next-Step Method

Assume the sale has been made and look past the commitment to the last actions that need to be taken. "When would you like for me to schedule the installation?"

The Opportunity Method

Present the customer with a brief window of opportunity when options are available. "You know that our prices increase in September. You want to get these lower prices now, don't you?"

The Weighing Method

If the customer still has second thoughts about making the purchase, show him or her how the return on investment outweighs the cost. "Let's weigh the ideas causing you to hesitate and the value you'll realize from going ahead."

After the Sale

Congratulations! You made the sale! Now it's time for that well-earned margarita, right? Yes! But you have more to do.

Customer service begins the moment someone becomes a customer. John Torre shares these tips for what to do after the sale.*

Keeping new customers depends on properly managing their expectations in order to keep them happy.

Although managing new customer expectations is not that difficult, it does take some time and effort by you and your employees to keep your new customers happy and placated.

Managing customer expectations begins with knowing what the customer will expect. To help you with your current—and future—customer base, here are nine key points that you will need to get right:

1. **People want you to show an interest in them.** You need to know not only about their business but who they are and the things they like and enjoy.

2. **People want you to respond fast.** Customers want their products and services "yesterday," not tomorrow or ten days from now. If you are slow, your customers will find someone else who can provide faster service.

3. **People want a live person to be available.** Your customers want to know they can immediately reach a live person when there is a problem or question. Provide numerous ways for your cus-

* John Torre, "Nine Customer Service Tips for after the Sale," Dale Carnegie Training of Central Ohio website, April 29, 2013: http://dalecarnegiewayohio.com/2013/04/29/nine-customer-service-tips-for-after-the-sale.

tomers to reach you, including business phone, home phone, fax, email, and cell phone.

4. **People want a friendly person to talk to.** No matter who talks with your customers, make sure that they are smiling on the phone. Even though customers can't see whom they're talking to, a smile helps to warm up a person's voice.

5. **Underpromise and overdeliver.** If you are overpromising and underdelivering on your products and services, we can assure you that your clients will NOT recommend you to anyone they know.

6. **Help your customer solve a problem.** If a customer calls you with a particular problem, they want you to help solve it. When you do that consistently, you will find yourself growing a large base of customers.

7. **Tell your customers, "Yes, I can do that."** Once you empower your staff to help your customers, you will find that not only are your customers happy but your employees are too.

8. **Don't nickel-and-dime your customers.** No matter what you sell, don't charge your customers for small or simple requests—it only makes you look cheap. Provide complimentary service whenever possible.

9. **Say "Thank you for your business."** Whenever you have a chance, let your customers know how much you appreciate their business. The key is conveying it with sincerity.

Remember: how customers perceive your business is their reality, so take a step back and examine how you do business. Additionally, you may want to consider emailing a customer-satisfaction survey to learn what you can do to improve your products and services.

These surveys can also be revenue generators for your business, because they are a great venue for asking your client base what other products or services they have an interest in learning more about.

Follow-up

If there's one thing you've learned in this book, sales is about becoming (say it with us now) a *trusted advisor* to your customers. In order to do that, call them back again after the sale. After all, what kind of trusted advisor disappears after she's made the sale? In fact, you might have noticed that our model is a cycle. *Confirm* leads back to *connect*.

Always follow up with your customers. You can create customer loyalty by providing exceptional value and following up to ensure that your solution has met the customers' expectations.

Stay in Touch

Effective follow-up involves contacting the customer after the sale to confirm that he or she is satisfied with the solution. Staying in touch goes beyond an isolated check-in: it aims to solidify and enhance your relationship with the customer. Remember to use social media!

Jonathan Vehar shares a story of the value of staying in touch. He says, "Several years ago, I worked with a client at a ski resort during an offsite retreat. I recently took my family to that same ski resort, and sent a note to this former client recalling the successful retreat at a very nice location, and thanking him for introducing me to this great ski area where my family had a great vacation. Now I had not been in conversation with this individual for a couple of years, and yet two weeks after sending that email to him, he sent me an inquiry about leading another offsite retreat for him. I did not know that he was preparing another retreat. I was not looking for the business opportunity, and yet this example speaks to the value of staying in contact to remind clients that you are available for your product or service. You never know when they will need what you have to offer, so stay on top of their minds even if you don't hear back from them time after time after time. You never know when you will hear back from them."

Ways to Stay in Touch

Michael Crom, Dale Carnegie & Associates Board of Directors, says, "Staying in contact with customers is an important way to increase your return on investment. Organizations of all sizes struggle to keep in touch with their customers, because it can be such a time-consuming experience. Setting up a simple follow-through system with your customers will allow you to keep your company's solution at the top of clients' minds when they are ready to buy." He gives these tips for staying in touch with customers after the sale.*

Schedule time for follow-up—and stick to it. We often don't make follow-through time a priority because it's time-consuming, and we have other, more pressing tasks to attend to. But it's important to set aside time in your schedule for it, as it is a long-term investment in your efforts, much as saving for retirement is in your personal life.

Take it slow. If you're worried about sounding pushy, just use the initial conversation to follow through. Don't make an offer the first time you call, and make it a point to circle back with that particular customer when you've built rapport with him or her.

Get organized. Customer-relationship management systems can be a great way to keep track of information. Always enter as many details as you can, completely and correctly, and use your follow-through time to make sure details are up-to-date and relevant.

In this chapter, we've covered ways for you to know when it's time to ask for the commitment. We also talked about several different ways to ask for the sale and looked at ideas for customer service, follow-up, and staying in touch. In the next chapter, we'll cover some troubleshooting tips for what to do if things didn't go quite as smoothly as you'd planned.

---

* "Sales Tips from the Vice President of Dale Carnegie Training," Dale Carnegie Training of Philadelphia website, June 28, 2011: http://www.dalecarnegiewayphilly .com/2011/06/28/sales-tips-from-the-vice-president-of-dale-carnegie-training/

The Bottom Line for Chapter 9

- Be aware of buying signals before you ask for the commitment.
- By using the power of observation, you can identify nonverbal body language signals that say if the prospect is interested or not.
- If you've successfully built the relationship, asking for or assuming the sale should be an easy next step.
- Customer service begins the moment someone buys your product or service.
- Following up with customers is essential for becoming a trusted advisor.
- Keeping in touch means developing a system for doing so.

10. DISASTERS, MISTAKES, AND CHALLENGES

Even the best salespeople make mistakes. Sometimes when mistakes happen during a sale, it's out of your control. Regardless of whose fault it is, the salesperson can make the biggest impact in resolving the problem.

How to Rescue a Client

Jonathan Vehar shares how you can use disasters as an opportunity to win a client's trust. In this sense, a salesperson can be considered the disaster quarterback who wins the game.

What do a bank, a glass manufacturer, and a baseball team have in common? When I worked in advertising, there were three opportunities where I had an opportunity to rescue a client's business. In two cases the agency had been a part of significant mistakes (that I had nothing to do with since I didn't work on the accounts). The senior leaders of the agency asked me to go to the client with them and sit down, listen to them, be yelled at by them, and then reassure them that we would do whatever it takes to make the job right. In both of these cases, we were able to fix the job, keep the client, and grow the business by demonstrating that we could be trusted to make it right.

In another situation, I led a project where the client was very unhappy with the result. I walked into the office one day and received a phone call that our client was driving two and a half hours to sit down, meet with us, and figure out how to fix it. My agenda for the day went out the window, and we pulled together the team to prepare. We chose to look at it as an opportunity to demonstrate to the client just how committed we were to their business. By bringing in the team with the client to sit down and work through the challenge, figure out how to fix it, and make sure that everybody was happy, we demonstrated just how important to the client was to the agency. Rather than losing the account that day, we cemented a relatively new client relationship that enabled the business to grow.

I'll never forget that there was construction going on in the office that day. Early in the meeting, while the client was emphatically and loudly (to be heard over the sound of the construction) telling us what we'd done wrong, a saw blade suddenly cut through the wall of the meeting room in which we were working. It startled all of us! Somebody made a remark about how this was rather indicative of the conversation that we were having, and it caused us all to laugh. The laughter broke the tension, and was critical to creating a collaborative environment that led to our future success.

If you handle mistakes successfully, the customer will be satisfied and is likely to buy again. When a customer comes to you with a complaint, follow these steps to ensure the mistake is handled proactively.

1. **Listen.** If you frequently experience the same complaint, it can become challenging to really listen. Nevertheless, give the customer an opportunity to vent frustration. Be empathetic. Listen for facts and feelings. Demonstrate proactive listening and resist the urge to respond too quickly.

2. **Question.** Begin in a friendly way. Ask questions to clarify the concern. Again, resist the urge to respond to the complaint until you truly understand the issue.

3. **Cushion.** Empathize with and find a point of agreement with the person. This does not necessarily mean you agree with the complaint, but it shows that you have heard and understand the importance of their concern.

4. **Address the issue.** Now that the emotional issues have been addressed, do everything in your power to resolve the practical aspects of the complaint. Take responsibility for the action, even if it wasn't directly your fault.

5. **Use questions.** Ask questions to test how well you have resolved the emotional and practical side of the complaint. Give the customer another opportunity to talk while you listen proactively.

6. **Offer additional help.** Turn the conversation away from the complaint by asking what else you can do for the customer. Try to provide something of value and truly *wow* the customer. Use mistakes as an opportunity to enhance the relationship and build customer loyalty.

7. **Follow up.** Often mistakes cannot be resolved completely on the first point of contact. If you need to get back to the customer, do so quickly and thoroughly. Even if you know the mistake has been resolved, create a reason to contact the customer. The customer relationship is key.

The Sales of the Future

Sometimes the challenge doesn't come in the form of a disaster or a mistake made by you or one of your team members. Sometimes the challenge is just the fact that the world changes and evolves.

At Dale Carnegie Training, we understand this as well. After all, a lot has changed since 1937. In order for our company to stay fresh and relevant, we needed to change and keep up with the times. When you Google our name, more than 7.5 million results come up. Why? Because we are keeping up with the times. We conduct primary research and publish videos and blogs; we have online trainings and webinars. We write books and articles, curate content, and run ads. It takes constant effort from our worldwide team members to stay fresh in the minds of people who want training.

The Challenges Headed Our Way

Pallavi Jha of Dale Carnegie India talks about coming challenges:

> We live in a time when our customers are buying things online. They have access to quick comparison shopping, quick fulfillment, and instant gratification. How do you become a trusted advisor when they are doing so much on their own? Knowledge-driven sales isn't enough. How do you differentiate when people can get all the information they need online?
>
> You have to find a way to make it relevant for *that* customer. They are looking for a personal touch. It has to become a service-oriented discussion. That's the only way that the average salesperson can keep from becoming a victim of the Amazon sales process.

Ask yourself, "Where are they in the customer journey, and how can I add trust and credibility to that part of the process?" How do we get involved at an earlier stage of decision making? Get involved in uncovering the need. If you can get at that stage, you'll have more influence.

The answer, of course, is asking the right questions. And that takes constant communication with the client. In the beginning, they can be learning what they need through you. You need to talk about emerging trends and advise. Or you need to be able to say, "She has already decided, so let's ask her some questions."

Salespeople tell me that one of their key challenges is how sophisticated the customer is today. How can we meet their expectations?

One way to do this is to make sure you have good intelligence on your customer and your products so that you can stay ahead of the curve. Technology and innovation are always changing. We now have virtual meetings and AI technology. There's always a calamity somewhere that people need to deal with. When you learn how to use technology well to become a trusted advisor to your customers, then you can stay ahead.

Another way is to help your customer use sales intelligence for themselves. How can they measure their own customer satisfaction? Surveys aren't enough.

The way to address the challenge of the sophisticated customer is to shift from chasing revenue and sales to looking at the holistic customer journey. Develop collaborative working relationships with other departments in your company. Get to know people in all departments, so that when mistakes happen, you can tell your customer, "Let me call my guy in shipping and see what's going on."

Doing this is essential to sales success, because if, for example, delivery is consistently late, then it becomes harder for you to sell.

The sales process is changing, and we're making the case that trust-based relationship selling is the only way to differentiate yourself and face the challenges ahead.

The Bottom Line for Chapter 10

- Every salesperson makes mistakes. It's not the mistake that is the problem; it's what you do after the mistake that matters.
- A problem is an opportunity to strengthen the relationship beyond what it was before the mistake happened.
- In order to avoid falling victim to the Amazon environment, continually look at where else to add value for your clients.
- The earlier you can get into the decision process, the more influence you will have.
- Using sales intelligence (and helping your customers to do the same) will help you stay ahead of the curve.
- Teaching is learning. Post your top takeaway from the chapter or from part 2 on social media.
- Always follow up with your customer.

*Thousands of salesmen are pounding the
pavements today, tired, discouraged, and
underpaid. Why? Because they are always
thinking about what they want. They don't
realize that neither you nor I want to buy
anything. If we did, we would go out and buy it.
But both of us are eternally interested in solving
our problems. And if a salesman can show us
how his services or his merchandise will help us
solve our problems, he won't need to sell us—
we will buy. And a customer likes to feel
that he is buying—not being sold.*
—DALE CARNEGIE,
HOW TO WIN FRIENDS AND INFLUENCE PEOPLE

Part Three

Winning the Mental
Game of Sales

11. WWDCD?

Why do we need to talk about winning the mind game of sales? One reason is that our research shows what you think about actually matters to buyers. Customers trust salespeople with confidence (71 percent) and a positive attitude (79 percent). In *Sell!* we have talked a lot about becoming a trusted advisor to your customers. We've given you a step-by-step system for developing and nurturing those relationships. But in the real world, where selling actually happens, it becomes less about the tools you've learned or the things you've practiced saying, and more about what you say to yourself. Sales is in the end a mind game between the salesperson and himself or herself. When you get in front of a prospect or customer, the words you say to yourself can make or break the sale.

We talked earlier about the power of questions when it comes to talking to a prospect or a customer. What about the questions you ask yourself? Those are even more powerful.

The Power of Self-Questions

Let's revisit the Questioning Model and apply the process to your self-talk. Recall the categories:

As-Is Questions

As-is questions help us determine the buyer's current situation. They give us a picture of key issues like product specifications, others who influence the buying decision, and challenges that we may be able to address in our solution.

Should-Be Questions

Should-be questions help us discover the buyer's vision of his or her operation at optimum performance. Questions here focus on how the situation could be different if we help the buyer solve their problems.

Barrier Questions

Barrier questions identify the factors that are stopping the buyer from achieving the should-be. While barriers are not objections, they can lead to objections. For example, a specified budget is a barrier that can lead to objections about price. Questioning should focus on how the return on investment can have a positive effect on the budget.

Payout Questions

Payout questions clarify how the buyer will personally benefit from the solution. Responses to these questions allow us to understand and appeal to the motivational reasons for buying.

Questioning Self-Talk

Now think about the kinds of questions you ask yourself in the areas, or the self-talk that may be helping or hindering you.

As-Is Questions

"Their boss doesn't even see the current problem. How am I even going to sell my solution when the key players won't even acknowledge there's a problem?"

Or "They don't even have a need for what I sell. They seem to be doing just fine with their current solution. What can I even add that's an improvement?"

Should-Be Questions

"You know what should be? I should have the resources I need to be able to make this sale. But with the cutbacks in our company, I'm not able to make the sales calls I need to be able to meet my quota."

Barrier Questions

"Our product is too expensive. We haven't kept up with the times, and customer budgets are shrinking. There's no way I can justify our prices."

Payout Questions

"Honestly, our solution barely even makes a difference. The same people keep doing the same things, and it doesn't matter if they use ours or a competitor's."

While these may be exaggerations, it's safe to say that most of use have thought similar things at one point or another. When you face rejection, don't feel you have the resources you need to do your job, or don't believe in your product 100 percent, it can be hard to walk in that room and put on a big smile.

What's a salesperson to do?

WWDCD?

This is the point in which you need to channel your inner Dale Carnegie. Ask yourself, "What would Dale Carnegie do?" If you could have a conversation with him about the challenges you're currently facing, the things that have you discouraged, or just to get some advice, what do you think he would say?

In all of his books, audios, and other writings, one of his key messages is that you should see yourself as the messenger of something important. It's about self-confidence.

How you show up in a sales situation reflects the value you believe you bring to the world. It has less to do with the copier toner you sell, or the shoes, or the software, and more to do with having the mind-set, "I am here to help. I have something valuable to offer." Stop seeing yourself as someone who sells and start focusing on serving the prospect. Focus on being—you guessed it—a trusted advisor.

Some people struggle with this. If they dig a little, they uncover the self-talk that says, "Who am I to come in here and tell them how I can make their lives better?" Or if they aren't fully passionate about the product or service they sell, they might have the belief, "This solution isn't even that valuable. I'm not even that comfortable selling it."

Here's an example from one of our trainers: "I have trained yacht brokers that sell very expensive and beautiful vessels. Almost every session, someone will come up front at a break and say, 'I'm not sure if this Hatteras 72 motor yacht is worth $3.4 million!' I always ask them, 'Do you know why they buy this type of product?' The typical answer is because they think they can, or they have a lot of money. Wrong! Usually they buy because they want to own superior quality, or want to have the family involved on this yacht at Christmas or when sailing the Caribbean. Family is an important driver for the decision. By interviewing a few current clients, you can find out why they buy, and it will dramatically increase your belief and confidence in yourself."

Those are the beliefs you need to identify and question in order to adopt the mind-set of a trusted advisor.

Robin James was an admissions counselor at a brand-new MBA program aimed at working adults. Her job was to give prospective students tours of the campus, ask questions that helped her identify the need, and then sell them a $12,000 one-year program.

The problem was, as she was working there, she stopped having confidence in the quality of the education. The classes offered were not typical for an MBA program, and there was a strong push for the professors to give good grades so that the program could receive accreditation. She didn't think that the information the students learned was what an MBA should know. But the admission standards were low, the tuition was very inexpensive compared to that of other programs, and the classes were easier than typical MBA classes.

Robin felt conflicted. Here she was in a sales position, but she didn't value what she was selling. So one night she had an imaginary conversation with Dale Carnegie.

"How can I sell a graduate program that I feel is sub-par?" she said in her mind.

"By shifting what you see as the value proposition," imaginary Dale said.

"What do you mean?"

"Robin, these people are not students who are going to get accepted into a traditional MBA program. Those programs are rigorous and very hard to get into. That isn't your competition. The value you're providing is a program that is easier to get into and easier to complete, and is designed for students whose choice is your program or no program. You're offering people a chance to get a graduate degree when they would not otherwise have the opportunity. Not every car buyer wants an expensive sports car. Some people want inexpensive transportation. Don't feel bad that you aren't selling sports cars to economy-car buyers."

You see, the mind-set of a trusted advisor is that you are helping the buyer uncover opportunities in areas that matter to *them*. You have the potential to add value by helping the other person find a solution to something that is important to them.

That's a pretty cool job to have, don't you think? So the next time someone asks you what you do for a living, you can just say, "I solve problems."

Field Notes

Since this is the field-guide portion of the book, write out your answers to the following questions.

When you encounter a salesperson, what is your first reaction? Is it "Go away?" Is it "Hey, me too?" Is it something else?

_____

_____

_____

_____

When you're not at work, what is your level of self-confidence? Through-the-roof positive? Don't want to get out of bed and face the world?

_____

_____

_____

_____

In an average conversation, how comfortable are you directly offering suggestions or advice? Why did you choose that answer?

_____

_____

_____

_____

Do you feel good about what you're selling? If not, what other value does your product or service (or your relationship with your customer) offer?

_____

_____

_____

_____

12. DON'T WORRY, SELL HAPPY

If you try honestly to see things from the other person's point of view, your positive, empathetic mind-set will fuel your success. Imagine selling sales training and hearing your prospect say this: "My customers only buy on price, so I'm not sure how you can help me and my team."

Here's how John Rodgers, Dale Carnegie's managing partner in Pittsburgh and Cleveland, responded. "Well, if you allow me to talk to your team and see if we can find ways to create a business case, perhaps we can win more business. He said, 'Be my guest.' By asking questions of him and his team, we discovered that to companies working on roads and bridges, downtime was the killer and was costly in their business model. In fact, equipment failure and downtime were two of the reasons why they might miss a time schedule, which would cost their organizations tens of thousands of dollars. We discovered that he was the only heavy-equipment dealer offering same-day road service to all equipment in a rather large regional territory.

"Then we trained their sales team through questioning to build this requirement into all equipment bids for purchasing new equipment. Their customers were excited, because having to pay a few more dollars on the front end to be assured the equipment was running and that jobs could be completed on time meant they would save costs and drive profits higher. Within two years the equipment dealership I was working with gained almost 90 percent of market share at high profits. This of course lasted until competitors adjusted their service capabilities."

But sometimes our day looks more like this: Just minutes into his sales call, Allen Sumpter heard the voice in his head: "He can tell I don't know what I'm talking about. You didn't do enough research before this meeting. You're blowing the sale."

Allen, like most of us, has an inner critic that provides an ongoing narrative, whether conscious or subconscious. Very often we are our own worst enemy. We worry about things that aren't real; we worry about things that we can't change, or that will never come to fruition.

Most of us choose to respond to this inner critic either by ignoring it or arguing back. But much like with the toddler who wants ice cream before dinner, that doesn't work very well. The voice just gets more and more demanding and loud.

Instead Dale Carnegie offers some basic techniques for fishing out the genuinely constructive things your inner worrywart has to say from the mean things, which sound as if they are being said by an angry parent.

Basic Techniques for Analyzing Worry

1. Get all the facts.
2. Weigh all the facts, then come to a decision.
3. Once a decision is reached, act!
4. Write out and answer the following questions:
   a. What is the problem?
   b. What are the causes of the problem?
   c. What are the possible solutions?
   d. What is the best possible solution?
5. How to face trouble:
   a. Ask yourself, "What is the worst that can possibly happen?"
   b. Prepare to accept the worst.
   c. Try to improve on the worst.

In other words, develop a compassionate new inner voice that can counter the critic. When you find yourself worrying or hear the negative voice beating you up, simply tell it, "Thank you. I appreciate your concern. You're right, I really could have prepared better for this meeting. But even if I lose the sale, I can still learn something. And I will have provided value in some way to the other person. Nothing is for naught."

FEEL Happy

Believe it or not, you can actually change your mood from one that is stressed out and anxious to one of confidence and happiness. The steps follow the acronym FEEL, which stands for *focus*, *eat*, *exercise*, and *love*.

Focus

What are you focusing on? Are you allowing yourself to think negatively without realizing it? Instead focus on positive things. Some days this is really hard, so pick something small. Look around the room right now. What is something positive you can find to focus on? It might be as simple as a text you got from your best friend this morning, your perpetually happy dog, or that invitation to a party this weekend. In any situation, you can find something to focus on that is positive. Doing so will switch off the negative neurochemicals in your brain and turn on the positive ones.

Eat

What you're eating or not eating can make a major impact on your mood. If you're attacked with a case of the blues, feeling down on yourself, feeling irritable or impatient, eat something. But of course *what* you eat is just as important. Don't hit the vending machine. Instead grab some complex carbs to naturally increase serotonin levels in the brain. What you're eating and when can make a huge difference in your mood.

Exercise

Blah, blah, blah. We bet you're sick of hearing this, but it's true. Exercise improves your mood. So if your mood is low, get moving. Go for a walk. Get outside in nature. Clean your garage. Get moving!

Love

Finally, if you just can't stop that nagging voice in your head, reach out to those you love. Not to complain, but to do something loving for someone else. Research shows that when people engage in altruistic behavior—doing something for someone else, just because—they actually feel better themselves.

In all, just remember. When your inner critic starts yelling, you need to listen to what it's telling you and then FEEL it.

Salespeople are always worried about hitting numbers and creating enough revenue. Some fall into the trap of trying to do more and more and get very unbalanced in their lives. To counteract this tendency, they need to set clear goals to reach, detail the activity required to reach these goals and closely monitor how they are doing. Don't forget to take time to celebrate at each milestone in order to allow yourself to reset for the next challenge!

13. DON'T SINK YOUR OWN SHIP

"I really should go to sleep," David Kristoff thought when he noticed that it was 12:30 a.m. "I have that presentation in the morning, and I need to leave the house by 7:30." But instead of turning off the television, he convinced himself that he wasn't ready to sleep yet and blamed his boss for not letting him leave the office early enough that day.

Sure enough, when his alarm went off at 6:30, he didn't even hear it. He did hear the second alarm at 6:45, but kept hitting the snooze button until 7:15. By that time, it was too late to shower, get breakfast, or do any of the other things that make a morning seem calm and unrushed.

Leaving late, he got stuck in more traffic than antici-pated and was ten minutes late to the client's office. He'd forgotten the power cord for his laptop and had to spend ten minutes accessing his PowerPoint from the cloud on one of the client's computers. After that embarrassing start, the meeting just went downhill from there. David was off his game and didn't make the sale.

Does this sound familiar? There are a myriad of reasons and ways that we sabotage ourselves. Here are the top five ways that a person can undermine his or her own success.

The Five Biggest Saboteurs

1. **Not knowing what your goals are.** Let's say you want to take a business trip—hit the road and sell some product. So you get in the car and start driving around. You don't have a particular destination in mind; you're just out there driving around, hoping to find someone who needs your product. Clearly that's not a good way to make sales. In order to make sales, you need a destination. Whom will you sell to? Where are they located? It's not about spending longer hours driving around in your car. Working harder at a poorly articulated goal is a form of self-sabotage, because when it doesn't work, you can just say, "I stink at sales."

2. **Not having a plan for what you're going to do.** This goes along with the first point. You may have the best-articulated goal in the world, but if you have no plan for how to achieve it, it's the same thing as sitting in the car in the parking lot. Most salespeople forget the importance of a sales-call plan and don't set clear goals of how they are going to advance the sale. To achieve

movement with a client, they need to focus on a clear outcome or next step and gain commitment for this. Of course, you've learned a comprehensive system now, so this isn't going to be an issue for you.

3. **Not sticking to your plan.** Here's the one that catches most people up. You can have a great goal and a perfect plan, but if you don't stick to it, you're not going to be successful. It's like the guy who says he wants to lose the flab and build muscle. He sets a clear goal, buys a bunch of books and food for the keto diet, and then finds himself in the drive-through lane of the fast-food place on his lunch break.

   What can you do about it? How can you do what you really need to be doing? It all comes down to the *shift*. The shift is that moment of transition when you go from doing one thing to the other. So you've made your ten cold calls for the morning as planned. Now what? This is the most critical moment in the day. You are most susceptible to self-sabotage in the moment of the shift. It's like a manual-transmission car: when you are shifting gears, there is a period of time when the gears are disengaged. This is when you need to go back to the plan. Ask yourself, "What is the most effective thing I can be doing right now to achieve my goal?" You get home from work, and you'd been planning to follow up with the client you met today. But a glass of wine and your couch start to look really good right now. That's when reviewing your plan can make the difference between sticking to it and not.

4. **Overplanning.** Does this mean you never deviate from the plan? Of course not. Sometimes spring fever hits, and you want to call off work and go to the park. Do it! All work and no play makes Jack a dull boy.

   But if you find yourself consistently blowing off your plans, it might mean that you have too much crammed in there. It's important to build in some things that are fun, relaxing, and unplanned. Time to revisit your daily schedule and take some stuff out.

5. **Personal time wasters.** Finally, everyone has their personal time wasters. Maybe it's Facebook or shopping on Amazon. It could be binge-watching Netflix. It's so easy to go down the rabbit hole of YouTube videos, where you started out Googling videos of Dale Carnegie and end up watching video footage of a guy on a streetcar in 1910. Interesting, but not a very good use of time. In fact, *Forbes* magazine says that when you get distracted, it takes approximately twenty-three minutes to get back on task.* Allowing yourself to waste this amount of time can substantially affect your career.

Dale Carnegie Training has identified several ways to help you decide how to spend your time. Again it's not about saying you should never spend an evening (or a weekend)

---

* Omar Tawakol, "The Importance of Workplace Attention—and How to Control Workplace Distractions," *Forbes* website, Jan. 22, 2019: https://www.forbes.com/sites/forbestechcouncil/2019/01/22/the-importance-of-attention-intelligence-and-how-to-control-workplace-distractions.

watching *Game of Thrones*. It's about what you do most of the time that matters.

Time Management: How to Prioritize

Time flies when you're having fun—or not. The key is to optimize your time, both professionally and personally, in a manner that will yield the ideal results. Following is a brief list designed to help you prioritize tasks and work efficiently.

1. **Record planned activities.** Make a list of everything that you must accomplish for the day and/or week in order to achieve optimum results.

2. **Determine primary goals.** List your primary goals for the day or the week.

3. **Consider the 80/20 rule.** Determine which 20 percent of activities will yield 80 percent of the results, bringing you closest to your goals. When we coach an executive or professional salesperson, we look very carefully at where their time is spent. We commit to focusing more time on productive activities and less time fighting fires. We also discuss the gravitational pull of urgent things that have small importance.

4. **Evaluate important versus urgent.** Determine which activities are important and which are imperative or even urgent. Consider how certain tasks affect others, and the consequences for failing to complete them.

5. **Rank.** Use a ranking system to begin planning. "A" tasks have high priority and must be completed immediately. "B" tasks are moderately important but can be done after the "A" tasks. "C" tasks are of low importance and can be tackled in your spare time.

6. **Create a schedule.** Establish deadlines for each task and estimate the time required to complete each task. Create a schedule and look for opportunities to multitask. For example, can you couple something of lesser priority with something of greater importance?

7. **Reevaluate and adjust goals.** Review your goals, envision the finish line, and adjust your plan.

8. **Purge and eliminate** those tasks on your list that remain at the bottom and from a realistic point of view will never get done.

AFTERWORD

SOME FINAL THOUGHTS

Good news: Your market needs you and your relationship-selling, principle-based approach! Our research across industries and companies of all sizes gives you the following stark reality: 71 percent of customers say they would rather buy from a salesperson they completely trust than one who gave them a lower price. But fewer than four in ten say they trust their salesperson most of the time.

Ironically, the best way to develop a sales relationship is to *stop selling*. Stop focusing on the bottom line. Instead focus on becoming a trusted advisor and having relationships with customers that allow you to add value to their lives. *SELL! The Way Your Customers Want to Buy* has taught you the time-honored principles of relationship building that are the legacy of our founder, Dale Carnegie, and using a process based on our latest research. You'll be able to have pride in your career choice, because you are a problem solver who is focused on nurturing a trusting relationship with someone who happens to be your customer.

> *Personally I am very fond of strawberries*
> *and cream, but I have found that for*
> *some strange reason, fish prefer worms.*
> *So when I went fishing, I didn't think about*
> *what I wanted. I thought about what they*
> *wanted. I didn't bait the hook with*
> *strawberries and cream. Rather, I dangled*
> *a worm or grasshopper in front of the fish*
> *and said: "Wouldn't you like to have that?"*
> *Why not use the same common sense*
> *when fishing for people?*
> —DALE CARNEGIE,
> *HOW TO WIN FRIENDS AND INFLUENCE PEOPLE*

Part Four

Bonus Material

SALES TIPS FROM DALE CARNEGIE

Here are nine sales tips based on the principles outlined by Dale Carnegie.*

Tip 1: Smile. Carnegie called it "a simple way to make a good first impression." Every business encounter—across the desk, at the customer's front door, and even on the telephone—should begin with a smile. "Actions," Carnegie noted, "speak louder than words. And a smile says, 'I like you.'"

Tip 2: Listen. Customers and clients want to hear what you have to say, but they want you to hear what *they* have to say first. Beyond that, consider this: how can you, as a sales

---

* Tim Parker, "Nine Sales Tips from Dale Carnegie," QuickBooks Resource Center website, accessed April 28, 2019: https://quickbooks.intuit.com/r/marketing/9-sales -tips-from-dale-carnegie.

rep, know what customers need if you don't give them a chance to tell you?

Tip 3: Arouse an "eager want." It almost sounds poetic. Carnegie cited Harry A. Overstreet as the originator of this idea. Overstreet said, "Action springs from what we fundamentally desire." If you own a bait store, understand that customers do not desire night crawlers; they desire to catch fish. Pitch accordingly.

Tip 4: Use names. Learn the names of your employees, your customers, and your prospects as they enter your sphere of business. After you learn those names, use them. Carnegie's principle here is simple: a person's name is, to that person, the sweetest and most important sound in any language.

Tip 5: Avoid arguments. This would seem to be almost a given, but far too many salespeople, perhaps in their zeal, engage in arguments with a customer who shows resistance or says he or she likes another brand. Carnegie said, "The only way to get the best of an argument is to avoid it." Be respectful of the customer's opinion. Do not argue, criticize, or condemn. You will have an opportunity to brag about your offering soon enough.

Tip 6: If appropriate, apologize. If, at any point in a sales transaction or pitch, you discover you have made an error, don't make excuses. Say you are sorry and do so emphatically, Carnegie said. Then move on. You may be surprised at how quickly the whole incident is forgotten. If you insist on building a case for why you erred, you'll only drag things out.

Tip 7: Let customers sell to themselves. In general, people do not like to be told what to do or what to buy. Provide information and be helpful, but let customers make the decision. You do this by asking questions and steering the conversation until customers realize that your product or service is the solution they've been looking for.

Tip 8: Ask what's in it for customers. When discussing your product, put it in terms that speak to your customers' interests. You may have the biggest, fastest, and most reliable product on the market, but unless customers see how it benefits them, you won't make sales.

Tip 9: Dramatize your ideas. This has less to do with human interaction and more to do with a flair for the dramatic. Do not be afraid to engage in a little showmanship, as long as it is honest and doesn't mislead people. For example, Carnegie tells the story of a cash-register salesman who told a grocer that the registers his store was using were so old that he was literally throwing money away. With that, the salesman threw a handful of coins on the floor. He got the sale.

FINAL EXAM

Rate yourself on how well you feel you've mastered understanding the following key concepts of *SELL!*

Credibility Statement

1 —————— 2 —————— 3 —————— 4 —————— 5

Did I even read this book?   Meh, I'm OK.   I'm a master.

Qualifying Questions

1 —————— 2 —————— 3 —————— 4 —————— 5

Did I even read this book?   Meh, I'm OK.   I'm a master.

Agenda Statement

1 —————— 2 —————— 3 —————— 4 —————— 5

Did I even read this book?   Meh, I'm OK.   I'm a master.

Manage Misperceptions

1 ——————— 2 ——————— 3 ——————— 4 ——————— 5

Did I even read this book?   Meh, I'm OK.   I'm a master.

Questioning

1 ——————— 2 ——————— 3 ——————— 4 ——————— 5

Did I even read this book?   Meh, I'm OK.   I'm a master.

Summary Statement

1 ——————— 2 ——————— 3 ——————— 4 ——————— 5

Did I even read this book?   Meh, I'm OK.   I'm a master.

Facts, Benefits, and Applications

1 ——————— 2 ——————— 3 ——————— 4 ——————— 5

Did I even read this book?   Meh, I'm OK.   I'm a master.

Evidence

1 ——————— 2 ——————— 3 ——————— 4 ——————— 5

Did I even read this book?   Meh, I'm OK.   I'm a master.

Trial Commitment

1 ——————— 2 ——————— 3 ——————— 4 ——————— 5

Did I even read this book?   Meh, I'm OK.   I'm a master.

Respond to Objections

1 ——————— 2 ——————— 3 ——————— 4 ——————— 5

Did I even read this book?   Meh, I'm OK.   I'm a master.

Paint a Word Picture

1 ——————— 2 ——————— 3 ——————— 4 ——————— 5

Did I even read this book?   Meh, I'm OK.   I'm a master.

Ask for a Commitment

1 ——————— 2 ——————— 3 ——————— 4 ——————— 5

Did I even read this book?   Meh, I'm OK.   I'm a master.

Follow Up/Stay in Touch

1 ——————— 2 ——————— 3 ——————— 4 ——————— 5

Did I even read this book?   Meh, I'm OK.   I'm a master.

Ask for a Referral

1 ——————— 2 ——————— 3 ——————— 4 ——————— 5

Did I even read this book?   Meh, I'm OK.   I'm a master.

Become a Trusted Advisor

1 ——————— 2 ——————— 3 ——————— 4 ——————— 5

Did I even read this book?   Meh, I'm OK.   I'm a master.

DALE CARNEGIE
SALES TOOL KIT

Unique Selling Proposition

Almost every product or service on the market today has competition. People may even believe your solution is interchangeable with what your competitors offer. *You* know what sets your solution apart, but does the customer? Having a strong understanding of your *unique selling proposition* (USP) will allow you to quickly explain why *your* solution is better than the rest.

Your USP should:
• Differentiate your solution from competitors'.
• Explain what you offer that others don't.
• Identify what makes your solution better.

Along with identifying the USP of your solution, consider what makes you unique as a salesperson. Write your own personal USP.
• Why are you great to work with?
• What is your personal differentiator?
• How will your attitude play a role?

Credibility Statement Worksheet

Prospect name:

Preapproach information:

1. Broad overview of benefits you provide:

_____

_____

_____

_____

2. Specific results of value you added for your clients:

_____

_____

_____

_____

3. Suggestion that similar benefits are possible:

_____

_____

_____

_____

4. Transition:

_____

_____

_____

_____

Appointment Power Phrase

To ask for the appointment, develop your own *appointment power phrase*. It looks like this:

1. Reason for contacting, tied to key issues.
2. Brief statement on how you are solving problems like theirs.
3. Ask for appointment, or ask for permission to ask questions.

Qualifying Questions

Once you've gained agreement to talk further, consider asking questions to see if you are speaking with a qualified customer. This will reduce the amount of time spent setting appointments with people who are unlikely to buy or don't have the authority.

There are five types of qualifying questions. The questions you ask will depend on your business. Whenever possible, your questions should be based upon your pre-approach research.

1. Permission Question

"Thanks for agreeing to meet with me. To see if we might have a good fit for you, can I ask you a few questions?"

2. Need Question

"I see from your website that one of your current initiatives is to . . . Are you currently purchasing to prepare for this?"

3. Quantity Question
"How much do you use . . . on a quarterly basis?"

4. Budget Question
"What kind of budget are you working with?" (This question can be a red flag for your customer. Don't ask it without first establishing trust and credibility, and try to find ways to get the information without asking it directly if possible).

5. Authority Question
"In addition to you, who else is involved in the decision-making process? Will you invite them to our meeting?"

Define the types of questions you would ask to your prospect, and then develop questions on the basis of these areas.

Question Type

_____

_____

_____

_____

Question Type

_____

_____

_____

_____

Question Type

_____

_____

_____

_____

Question Type

_____

_____

_____

_____

Question Type

_____

_____

_____

_____

Questioning Model

Develop your own questions for each of the type of questions:

Payout

_____

_____

_____

_____

_____

Should-Be

_____

_____

_____

_____

Change

_____

_____

_____

_____

As-Is

_____

_____

_____

_____

Trial Close

Write out several trial close statements that feel comfortable to you:

Trial Close 1

_____

_____

_____

_____

Trial Close 2

_____

_____

_____

_____

Trial Close 3

_____

_____

_____

_____

Trial Close 4

_____

_____

_____

_____

Painting a Word Picture Worksheet

Customer:
Primary Interest:
Individual Motive:

1. Remind the customer that he or she lacks the benefit of your solution and get agreement.

_____
_____
_____
_____

2. Remind the customer that your solution will fulfill that benefit.

_____
_____
_____
_____

3. Paint a word picture.

_____
_____
_____
_____

4. Ask for a commitment.

_____
_____
_____
_____

The Magic Formula Worksheet

Story 1

Incident

_____

_____

_____

_____

_____

Action

_____

_____

_____

_____

Benefit

_____

_____

_____

Story 2

Incident

_____

_____

_____

_____

_____

Action

_____

_____

_____

_____

Benefit

_____

_____

_____

Story 3

Incident

_____

_____

_____

_____

_____

Action

_____

_____

_____

_____

Benefit

_____

_____

_____

Story 4

Incident

_____

_____

_____

_____

_____

_____

Action

_____

_____

_____

_____

Benefit

_____

_____

_____

Story 5

Incident

_____

_____

_____

_____

_____

Action

_____

_____

_____

_____

Benefit

_____

_____

_____

Gaining-Commitment Worksheet

Although it may be uncomfortable to ask for the commitment, if you have successfully built the relationship, asking for the purchase should be an easy step. Use a method that feels natural.

Direct Question
Often the best way to gain commitment is to ask for it: "Are you ready to go ahead with this decision now?"

_____

_____

_____

_____

Alternate-Choice Method
Ask the customer to select one of two options.

_____

_____

_____

_____

Minor-Point Method
Call on the customer to make a minor decision that indicates that the larger buying decision has been made.

_____

_____

_____

_____

_____

Next-Step Method
Assume the sale has been made and look past the commitment to the last actions that need to be taken.

_____

_____

_____

_____

_____

Opportunity Method
Present the customer with a brief window of opportunity when options are available.

_____

_____

_____

_____

_____

Weighing Method
If the customer still has second thoughts about making the purchase, show him or her how the return on investment outweighs the cost: "Let's weigh the ideas causing you to hesitate and the value you'll realize from going ahead."

_____

_____

_____

_____

_____

Asking for Referrals Worksheet

Opening

Reconnecting the customer with their specific benefits. "I'm glad we were able to help your team improve productivity, reduce silos, and reduce conflict."

_____

_____

_____

_____

Options for Requesting a B2B Referral

Others with similar issues:

"Communication problems are often widespread throughout an organization. What other departments could benefit from improved communication?"

_____

_____

_____

_____

Support your organization:

"I know you want to get more recognition from your executive team. Being able to offer a solution to a key organizational issue could increase your profile."

_____

_____

_____

_____

Organizational impact:

"What kind of a difference would it make if other departments were operating at the same level that your team is now?"

_____

_____

_____

_____

_____

Options for Requesting a B2B Referral
Describe your customer profile.

"In general, we work with people who are looking to . . ."

_____

_____

_____

_____

_____

"Who comes to mind?"

_____

_____

_____

_____

_____

Closing

Ask for an introduction.

"Could you call them in advance so that they know I'll be reaching out?"

_____

_____

_____

_____

Your Turn

Opening

_____

_____

_____

_____

Referral Request

_____

_____

_____

_____

Closing

_____

_____

_____

_____

INDEX

Printed in the USA
CPSIA information can be obtained
at www.ICGtesting.com
JSHW012023140824
68134JS00033B/2847